How to Be a Stoic When You Don't Know How

Ten easy exercises at The Stoic Gym

Dr. Chuck Chakrapani

The Stoic Gym Publications

THE STOIC GYM

www.TheStoicGym.com

How to Be A Stoic When You Don't Know How/ Chuck Chakrapani. —1st
ed.
ISBN 978-0-920219-69-0

Contents

How to Be a Stoic

Your roadmap

There is a huge community of modern Stoics. The Stoicism Facebook group has over 50,000 members. The largest group of Stoics that ever comes together in one place happens every year at Stoicon, the annual Stoic conference. More than 5,000 people enroll in Stoic Week (a one-week online training) every year.

Yet learning about Stoicism, joining the Facebook group, attending Stoicon, and the like are not enough to attain the benefits of Stoicism. We need a clear roadmap, an action plan, and an overall idea of our journey.

Why we need a guide

Even though Stoicism has been around for over 2,300 years, practically everything that the early Stoics wrote for the first three hundred years is lost. All we have left are the writings of three prominent Stoics who lived three hundred years later: Seneca, Epictetus, and Marcus Aurelius (plus, some of Musonius Rufus' lectures). Even these writings are incomplete. So, we need to reconstruct Stoicism from secondary writings of the later Stoics and from the writings of the later Stoics. It is difficult to know where to begin. A clear guide to Stoicism, even if it is not perfect, is a good place to start. Once we have the basics in place it is easy to build upon them. That's where this book comes in.

What does this book aim to do?

A clear roadmap

We may know a lot about Stoicism and yet not have a clear roadmap for achieving the Stoic goal of a life that runs smoothly. When we say that we don't have the time to practice something, it is often because we don't have clarity on how to practice. Our journey seems hard when we are not sure of the path to take. We stand confused at every fork in the road. But if we have a roadmap, we spend less time in confusion, second guessing ourselves and wondering whether we have taken the right turn.

Stoic concepts such as "living according to nature" or "practicing wisdom," etc. may mean different things to different people. What do they really mean in everyday life? How does one practice these precepts?

Without a clear roadmap, it is easy to lose our way. As Seneca says,

> We blunder along and never stop, or even watch our step. But surely you can see how crazy it is to rush ahead in the dark ... we continue to move as fast as we can in the direction we are already going.
>
> Seneca, *Moral Letters*, 3

So, the first purpose of this book is to provide you with a clear roadmap, saving you time and confusion.

The core of Stoicism

When we strip away the complexity that envelops Stoicism, we will see its fundamental concepts are not difficult to understand. At its very core is a simple model of how happiness (*eudemonia*) works. We all look for happiness. But how do we create happiness? What is the raw material we need to work on? The Stoics said the only raw materials we have to create our happiness are our "impressions." What are impressions? Impressions are the way we perceive the world. Suppose someone calls you stupid. Your impression could be one of many:

- It is harsh
- He insulted me

- I don't deserve this
- She is clueless

Throughout the day and through the night we are bombarded with impressions: The room is hot, the room is cold, I am going to be late, she is rude, I am hungry, she is generous, I am not well, and so on. Some of these impressions are true, others are false. But all we have in life are impressions. How we use them will decide whether we achieve happiness or not. If we judge our impressions the correct way, they will lead to happiness.

But how to judge our impressions the right way? The Stoics said that, to judge impressions correctly, we need four special skills, which they called "virtues." These special skills are:

1. **Wisdom**: Knowing what to do and what not to do under any conditions.
2. **Justice:** Knowing what belongs to whom and giving everyone their due.
3. **Moderation**: Knowing what to select and what to avoid.
4. **Courage**: Knowing what is terrible and what we should be afraid of and what is not terrible and what we should not be afraid of.

They said that to develop these four special skills, you need to practice three disciplines: The discipline of assent, the discipline of desire, and the discipline of action.

FOUR SPECIAL SKILLS
Wisdom, Justice
Moderation, Courage

IMPRESSIONS → JUDGMENT → EUDEMONIA The Good Life

THREE DISCIPLINES
Assent, Desire, Action

Figure 1 The Stoic model of happiness

As you practice the four virtues and the three disciplines, you will be participating in the festival of life. This is the core of Stoicism (unless you want to be a Stoic scholar).

A clear action plan

Studying exercise physiology won't build muscles. You need to act—like going to the gym and lifting weights. Similarly, just reading a lot about Stoicism will not make you happy. You must act. You must practice and build your Stoic muscles.

Every habit is formed, and every capacity strengthened, by our doing things associated with it. Walking makes you walk better, running makes you run better.

Want to be a reader? Read. Want to be a writer? Write. Go for a month without reading, you will see the effect. Lie down for ten days and then try to get up and walk, you'll see how weak your legs have become. So, if you want to do something, make it a habit.

Epictetus, *Discourses* 2.18,1-5 (Chuck Chakrapani *Stoic Choices*, Ch. 18)

So, the second purpose of this book is to provide you with a specific action plan which you can follow for the next ten weeks to make your learnings become habits.

Special features of the book

The book is written in plain English. It is built around 10 big Stoic ideas and covers every important tenet of Stoicism (see next section). It has been field-tested by our group of volunteers, the Stoic Street Irregulars.
- Every subsection of the books is supported by a Stoic quote.
- Every lesson is supported by specially curated Stoic readings.
- Every lesson is reinforced by a carefully crafted exercise.

A preview of the journey

This course is an action plan for living a happy life using Stoic principles. It is based on what I believe to be the most fundamental precepts of Stoicism.

Figure 2 Four steps to living a happy life

1. **Understand the foundations of Stoicism.** Understand the basic principles on which Stoicism rests.
2. **Develop the needed knowledge and skills.** Learn how to get the special knowledge we need to live a rational life. (Stoic special knowledge consists of the virtues: wisdom, justice, moderation, and courage.)
3. **Practice the needed disciplines.** Learn how to practice the three disciplines needed to achieve happiness. (The three Stoic disciplines: assent, action, and desire.)
4. **Live effectively every day.** How do we handle our negative emotions which seem to overtake us even when we try to act rationally? Enjoy the festival of life. How do we embrace life and make it as enjoyable as possible instead of just avoiding suffering?

The course outline

The course is built on the following themes.

The foundational principles of Stoicism

1. We are unhappy because of the way we think.
2. Our life will flow smoothly when we live according to nature.

3. Ignore what is not under your control.
4. Act on what is under your control.

Four special skills we need to practice Stoicism

1. Wisdom   What to do and what not to do
2. Justice   Who does it belong to and who does it not belong to
3. Moderation What to select and what not to select
4. Courage   What is terrible and what is not terrible

Three disciplines we need to develop

1. The discipline of assent
2. The discipline of desire
3. The discipline of action

How to live a Stoic life

Being Stoic in everyday life
Enjoying the festival of life

The house metaphor

Figure 3 The house metaphor with 4 foundations, four walls,
three windows and two sloping roofs

In this course I will use a simple house as a metaphor. Think of:

- The four foundational principles as the foundations going in four directions.
- The four walls of the house as the four special skills or virtues; the three windows on the walls are the three disciplines.
- The roof sloping in two directions as the way we should live every day.

How to use the course

We have made this course as simple as possible, so you don't have to be confused about what to do next or even set aside too much time to practice. All you need to do is:

1. On the first day of the week (let's assume it's Sunday) you read the sections for that week: The Lesson, Selected readings, Exercise for

the week. Highlight or underline all important parts. This may take an hour or so.

2. Every day of the week read the quote of the day and remember it several times during the day. Practice the exercise for that week. The exercises can be done as you go about your daily life. You don't have to set aside any special time for this.

3. During the week, reread the underlined and highlighted parts to remind yourself of the lesson.

4. Do 1 to 3 above for the next ten weeks.

This is all that is needed to succeed.

A Very Short Summary of The Course

The purpose of this course is to train you to live a life that flows smoothly.

Ask this single question, whenever you are worried, upset, or angry about something:

Is this thing under my control?

NO—If it is NOT under your control, it is nothing to you. Don't worry about it.

YES—If it is under your control, ask four questions about your next action:

- Is it unwise?
- Is it unjust?
- Is it excessive?
- Is it terrible?

If it is unwise, unjust, excessive, or terrible, don't do it.

If it is wise, just, moderate and courageous, act on it.

Learn how to let go of everyday problems and enjoy life.

That is all.

This training program expands on this and explains how and why this will lead you to a life of happiness, freedom, and tranquility.

PART I

THE FOUNDATIONS

What is happiness? The Stoics defined happiness as the good flow of life. Happiness follows when we live according to nature. When we live according to nature, we are not in conflict with ourselves or with reality.

Our thoughts create our unhappiness. By changing our thoughts, we can go from unhappiness to happiness.

Our problems are due to our mistaken judgments of things. If we want to be happy, we need to judge things correctly and take total control over how we judge things.

To judge things correctly, we need to realize that we have total control over certain things but not over other things. We need to limit our actions to things that are in our total control. We should stop worrying about things that are beyond our control.

These are foundational principles of Stoicism.

Foundation 1. How to Create a Life That Flows Smoothly

Lesson 1

The big idea 1. Happiness is a good flow of life

The goal of Stoicism is happiness; living the good life.

What is happiness? Zeno of Citium, the founder of Stoicism, defined happiness as "a good flow of life." A good flow means that our life runs smoothly, so we are in harmony with ourselves and with the way things are.

Our life flows smoothly when we "live in accordance with nature." Our actions should be in harmony with our nature (who we are) and with the nature of the world (what the world is.) What is our nature? Our nature is rationality. What is the nature of the universe? The nature of the universe is the way things are. So, a happy life is a rational one that is in line with reality.

> Happiness is a good flow of life... The end may be defined as life in accordance with nature or, in other words, in accordance with human nature as well as that of the universe.
>
> Zeno, *Stobaeus*, ii.7

The cause of our mistaken judgments

It is not the things that happen to us but our judgments about them that cause us problems. We suffer when we believe we are reacting to events when we are actually reacting to our judgments about them. When we are wrong in our judgments, we create problems for ourselves. We get unhappy, anxious, worried, upset, annoyed or fearful. In this training session, we will look more closely at what is behind our confused judgments.

What is the reason we assent to anything? The fact that it appears to us to be so.

Epictetus, *Discourses* 1.28.1 (Chuck Chakrapani, *Stoic Foundations*, Ch. 28)

A life that flows well

"A good flow of life" is a life without constant friction, a life that runs smoothly.

For many of us, life doesn't flow smoothly. Sometimes it is because of a major problem: you have lost your job; you are going through a divorce, or you are diagnosed with a serious disease. Even when we don't have any major problem, we still face endless minor problems every day, "Why is it raining on today of all days, when I'm having an outdoor party?" "I wonder what he meant by that," "I should have remembered to do x or y," "The metro is too crowded," "She is always so rude," "The restaurant prices are a rip off." The list goes on and on.

These may be minor problems, but they compromise our happiness. They are small potholes as we drive on the highway of life. They make our life less enjoyable. We can't put our finger on why, but we know that our life doesn't flow as smoothly as it could. For most of us living life is serious business. We have to be careful. We fret. We get annoyed. We worry. We regret. We wish things were different. Our life is full of barely noticeable discomforts that collectively make our life run less smoothly.

And when we consciously notice a few things that go wrong, we tend to extend our discomfort to the entire day and to everything: "Today, nothing is going right!" and go looking for even more discomfort.

Is there a better way to live? Can we drive on a highway of life where the traffic flows smoothly with no speed bumps or potholes? Can we live without "problems"—big or small? Stoicism says yes and offers an alternative way of looking at things, a better way to live. It makes the bold claim that it is possible to live a life that flows smoothly, a life of freedom, as described by Epictetus:

> You are free when you live as you wish; when you cannot be compelled, obstructed or controlled; your choices cannot be blocked; when you get your choices fulfilled and when you face nothing that you want to avoid.
>
> Epictetus *Discourses* 4.1.1 (Chuck Chakrapani *Stoic Freedom*, Discourse 1)

What does it mean to live in accordance with nature?

A life that flows smoothly is a life that is "in accordance with nature"? What does that mean? Let's start with the idea that our life shouldn't be a struggle with ourselves, with others, or with the way things are. A life well-lived is not conflicted. Such a life is said to be "in accordance with nature."

To live in accordance with nature we have to live in harmony at two levels: internally and externally. Our actions should be in harmony with *our* nature (who we are) and with the nature *of the world* (what the world is).

1. **Living in harmony with our nature.** What is our nature? We are not distinguished from other animals by our physical prowess. We cannot fly like an eagle, pounce like a tiger, hop like a kangaroo, swim like a fish, run like a rabbit, or hunt like a lion. And yet we dominate this earth. How? Because of our ability to reason, something that no other animal does so well. This is what distinguishes

us the most from other animals. This is our nature. Therefore, living in accordance with our nature means living a life of reason, a life of rationality. Over this we have control.

2. **Living in harmony with the nature of the universe.** It is not enough to live in accordance with our nature. We should also live in harmony with the world outside (the universe). So, what is the nature of the universe? The nature of the universe is what is—the totality of what is happening, what we call reality. We have no general control over reality: earthquakes, storms, famine, people dying, our loved ones getting sick, delayed flights, who wins elections, and the like. We don't control these events. They are a part of reality. To be in harmony, we shouldn't mentally struggle against them. This doesn't mean that we are always passive. We may well act to try to influence the future course of events, based on our understanding of what has already occurred. But we do so without engaging in a losing internal battle against the reality of those events. Such struggles are pointless because facts are facts and we cannot change them.

To live in accordance with nature means we live a life of reason, while accepting reality of things and events around us as they are. When we don't live this way, our life does not flow well, because we are obstructing it by our irrationality and our refusal to see reality as it is.

I will not become an obstacle to myself.

Agrippinus, Quoted by Epictetus *Discourses* 1.1.28
(Chuck Chakrapani *Stoic Foundations*, Discourse 1)

How to live according to nature

So, to create a life that flows well we need to live according to nature. This means we should live a *rational life* that *does not conflict with reality*. What does that mean in practice? What defines a rational life? How do we avoid conflicts with reality? What is the touchstone that will tell us whether we are living according to nature?

We can identify everything that happens as either under our control or not under our control. If you want to be happy, that is under your control. If you want everyone in the world to be happy, that is not under your control. If you want to be kind to someone, that is under your control. If you want someone to be kind to you, that is not under your control.

If we examine things that we do or do not control, we will see that we control everything that comes from us: how we feel about things, what we agree to or disagree with, whether we want to act one way or another—what we call *the internals*. We don't control what happens in the natural world; how others think, feel and act; whether it rains or shines; whether your spouse will divorce you or not; whether our loved ones live or die—what we call *the externals*.

A rational person is aware of this distinction and confines his thoughts and actions to what is under his control, the internals. This is rationality.

The second part of this is to avoid conflict with reality (that is, the universe as it is.) Since reality is not under our control, we accept the way things are. When we accept reality as it is—including accidents, natural disasters, and personal tragedies—then we are not in conflict with the universe. (Again, this does not mean that we don't act. We do, and we will come back to this later.)

In the next few training sessions, we will expand on this theme and give practical guidelines to living according to nature to create a life that flows well. Although we talk about everyday life, the same principles apply even when you face more tricky situations in life, such as losing a job, going through a divorce, or being diagnosed with some serious illness. This will become obvious as we go through the course.

We must do what follows from nature ...We should neither miss noticing what nature expects of us nor accept anything that conflicts with it.

Epictetus *Discourses* 1.26.2 (Chuck Chakrapani, *Stoic Foundations*, Ch.26)

Key takeaways

1. *The goal of Stoicism is happiness or a life that flows smoothly.*
2. *We create a life that flows smoothly when we live according to nature.*
3. *Living according to nature means two things:*
   a. *Living a rational life—understanding what is under our control and acting on what is under our control.*
   b. *Accepting reality—understanding what is not under our control (the world as it is presented to us) and not getting upset about it.*

Selected readings. Week 1

What did the Stoics know that we don't?

[FROM Chuck Chakrapani, *Unshakable Freedom* Ch. 2]

What did the Stoics know about personal freedom that we don't? They knew that, "no great equipment should be necessary for happiness... External things are of very little importance." (Seneca, *Moral Essays*) They taught us that you can be completely free if you live according to nature. You can be free no matter what. It doesn't matter if you are rich or poor, healthy or ill, young or old, educated or uneducated, have power or have no power.

Understand What Is in Your Power

[FROM Epictetus *Discourses*, 1, Chuck Chakrapani *Stoic Foundations*, Ch 1)]

Reason, our best gift

If you are writing a letter to a friend, grammar will tell you how to write correctly, but not whether you should write that letter. If you study music, music will tell you whether something is melodious, but not whether it is proper to sing now. It is so with all disciplines. They cannot judge themselves. What can? The faculty of reason can.

Reason alone can understand and judge itself: what it is, what it is capable of, and the power it has. It can also pass judgment on other disciplines. What else tells us that gold is beautiful? What else can judge music, grammar, and other arts and tell us when and how to use them? Not the gold or the grammar, but the faculty that evaluates such impressions—reason. Only reason can judge music, grammar, and other arts, evaluate their benefits, and tell us when and how to use them.

So, it is fitting that God has given us control over this excellent faculty—and only this faculty—that rules over all others: the ability to interpret impressions correctly. Why are the other faculties not placed under our power? We would have been given power over other faculties too, but we are on earth and bound to a physical body and material things. Therefore, we cannot avoid being limited by external things. Even our bodies are not truly our own, but just cleverly constructed to seem that way. Given these limitations, it is as if the God, because he could not give us control over our body, making it free of restraint, has given us a portion of himself.

Reason gives us the ability to act or not act and to desire something or move toward or away from it by properly judging our perceptions or impressions. If we pay attention to just this one thing, we will never be hindered, and we will never complain, flatter, or find fault. Does this seem like a small gift to you? Of course not!

Don't burden yourself with concerns

But instead of doing just this one thing right—managing impressions to arrive at the right conclusion—we burden ourselves with many things: Our body, our possessions, our brother, friend, child, and the like. We concern ourselves with so many things that they weigh us down. So, when bad weather prevents us from sailing, we become anxious and start fretting about reality:

"What wind is it?"

"North wind."

"When will west wind blow?"

"When it chooses, my good friend. You don't control winds."

"What should we do then?"

"Make the best use of what lies within our power and deal with it according to its nature."

Don't add misery to what is happening

"But what if my life is being threatened and I am alone?"

"Do you want everyone's life threatened, too? Remind yourself what is in your power and what is not. I should die; should I die groaning, too? I am put in chains; should I feel miserable, too? I am deported; what keeps me from going with a smile on my face?"

Face whatever happens

Whatever is within our power, no one can take away.

"Tell me your secrets."

"I refuse." This is in my power.

"I will restrain you."

"Only my legs. Even God cannot take away my choice."

"I will throw you in prison."

"Only my body."

"I will behead you."

"Did I ever claim that mine is the only head that cannot be cut off?"

That is the attitude you should cultivate if you would like to be a philosopher. This is what you should think, write about, and practice every day. [Roman Senator] Thrasea used to say, "I would sooner be killed today than deported tomorrow."

What did [the Stoic philosopher] Musonius tell him? "If you choose death because it is the worse of the two, how foolish! If you choose it as a lesser evil, who put you in charge of that choice?"

It is foolish to have a preference when it is not under your control. Instead why don't you train yourself to be content and deal with whatever happens?

Don't become an obstacle to yourself

[The Stoic philosopher] Agrippinus said, "I will not become an obstacle to myself."

On hearing that he was being tried in the Senate, Agrippinus said, "Hope it turns out in my favor. But it is five o'clock. Time for my workout and bath."

Off he went to do his workout. When he was done, a friend came to inform Agrippinus that he was convicted.

"Death or exile?"

"Exile"

"What about my property?"

"You get to keep it."

"Let's go to Aricia and dine there."

This is how you should train yourself to think. When you think this way, what you desire cannot be restrained and what you want to avoid cannot be forced upon you.

"I must die. If now, I will die now. If later, I will dine now because it is dinner time. How? Like a person giving back what is not his own."

Exercise 1. Friction Finder

Read and understand this exercise fully and mentally rehearse the situations where you could use it. You will be using it every day for the rest of the week.

When to use it

The purpose of this week's workout is to make you conscious of the many minor (some major) irritations and annoyances you face throughout the day. You may be so accustomed to them that you are not even aware of them anymore. At this stage, it is not important to change your thinking or behavior. All you need to do is notice how often you feel mild—barely noticeable—discomfort during any given day.

Use this workout throughout this week as often as possible. If you are like most people, you will have scores of opportunities to practice throughout the day. At the end of the day, before going to bed, ask yourself how many times you remembered to practice today. If you had not practiced many times, mentally go over the day and name situations where you could have practiced it.

How it works

- Carry a pocket counter (which you can probably buy very cheaply in a dollar store) with you all day. If you don't want to buy a counter, carry a small notebook.
- Throughout the day, whenever you feel any discomfort coming on—even if is very minor—click the counter (or tally it in your pocket notebook). Do this right away, or as soon as you can after that.
- Watch your thoughts around them. See what you are telling yourself.

- If you feel that something that happened shouldn't have happened (or something that hasn't happened should have happened), you are not in accordance with reality or the universe.
- If you feel that somebody's behavior or something that happened is the cause of your annoyance, you are not in accordance with your nature.

Here are few examples:

Situation	Your thoughts
Your friend said something rude to you.	*She shouldn't have been rude to me.*
Someone is talking loudly over the phone in a quiet restaurant.	*It annoys me when people are so inconsiderate.*

Such thoughts create friction. Think about them as they happen. See whether you are not in line with the nature of the universe or not in line with your nature.

In the first example, your friend was rude to you. You are upset because you tell yourself, "She shouldn't have been rude." You are *not* in control of your friend's behavior. *Your thinking is not in accordance with the nature of the universe.*

In the second example, you are annoyed because someone is talking loudly on the phone when you want to enjoy a quiet meal. But to feel annoyed or not *is* under your control. For example, instead of feeling annoyed, you can choose to ignore him and concentrate on enjoying your meal. To feel miserable or not is your choice. *Your reaction is not in accordance with your nature because you are acting helpless._*Remind yourself that it is your choice to get annoyed or ignore the other person.

Additional comments

In many cases, our behavior may conflict with the nature of the universe as well as with our own nature.

At bedtime, review the day and see how often you conflicted with your own nature or the nature of the universe. If you did not do this exercise many times during the day, it is likely that you forgot about it or did not notice your annoyances during the day. If so, go through the different situations that you were in during the day and recall how you felt. Were you in accordance with nature 100 percent? If not, why were you upset, annoyed, or irritated? Was the conflict with yourself, with the universe, or with both?

Realize every single friction in your life is the result of your conflicting with nature. Bring yourself in line with nature for a happy, free, and peaceful life.

Daily quotes. Week 1

Sunday

Harmony makes small things grow, and a lack of harmony makes great things decay.

Seneca, *Moral Letters*, 3.41

Monday

Whatever happens, let your mind suppose it was bound to happen, and do not rail at nature.

Seneca, *Moral Letters*, 107, 9-10

Tuesday

Don't wish for things to happen the way you like them to. Rather, welcome whatever happens. This is the path to peace, freedom, and happiness.

Epictetus, *Enchiridion*, 8 (Chuck Chakrapani, *The Good Life Handbook,* Ch. 8)

Wednesday

The law of life ... we should do what nature demands.

Epictetus, *Discourses*, Chapter 1.26.2 (Chuck Chakrapani, *Stoic Foundations,* Ch. 26)

Thursday

Don't say "How unlucky that this has happened to me!" Say instead "How lucky that this has left me without bitterness!" M4.49

M. Aurelius, *Meditations*, 5.49 (Chuck Chakrapani, *Stoic Meditations*, Ch. 4.49)

Friday

Avoiding others is not possible. Nor do we have the power to change others. Then how do we deal with them? By understanding that people will act as the please, but we will act in accordance with nature.

Epictetus, *Discourses*, I.12.18-19 (Chuck Chakrapani, *Stoic Foundations*, Ch. 12)

Saturday

What is the penalty for not accepting things the way they are? To be just the way you are: miserable when alone and unhappy when with others. There is no need to throw you in prison, you already are in one.

Epictetus, *Discourses*, I.12.21,22 (Chuck Chakrapani, *Stoic Foundations*, Ch.12)

Foundation 2. Our Thoughts Create Our Unhappiness

Lesson 2

The big idea 2. Our thinking causes our unhappiness

All of us want to be happy. Yet very few of us are genuinely happy. Why? We are unhappy because we misunderstand the cause of our unhappiness. As a result, we manipulate the wrong things which often results in even more unhappiness. It is like believing the gas pedal in your car is the brake pedal. By pressing what you think is the brake, you are speeding up. Stoic principles show how to diagnose our problems the right way, so we can get rid of them and be happy no matter what we face right now or in the future.

People are not disturbed by things that happen, but by their opinion of these things.

Epictetus *Enchiridion,* 5 (Chuck Chakrapani, *The Good Life Handbook*, Ch.5)

The way we look at things

The ancient Stoics were philosophers of happiness. We are unhappy, they said, because our thinking is flawed. Life is not designed to be a struggle. Once we correct our errors in thinking and judge everything correctly, all our problems will disappear. We need to bring our thinking in line with who we are and how the world is.

Let us start with trivial things that cause us to be unhappy. Your favorite cup breaks and you are upset. Someone is texting while crossing the street and bumps into you and you are angry—"Why can't they look at where they're going?" Your new car has a scratch and you are disturbed. There's a traffic jam and you are worried because you are going to be late for a meeting. We believe that external things such as the cup breaking, the person who doesn't look where he is going, and the traffic jam caused us to be unhappy.

What happened	How we react
Our favorite cup breaks	We are upset
Someone bumps into us	We are angry
There's traffic jam	We are worried

When we assume that external things *cause* our unhappiness, it means that we believe we are helpless, and we are forced to react mechanically to external things like a robot. Is this true? Are we helpless? Not everyone is unhappy when a cup breaks, when someone bumps into them, or when they are in a traffic jam. If external events by themselves can cause our problems, everyone should be made equally happy or equally unhappy by the same things. But it is not so. Some people become distressed by these things and others shrug them off and go about their lives as if nothing had happened. So, external events by themselves do not make anyone unhappy.

The results you get are solely based on the cause—your opinion. You are the master of your opinion. It has nothing to do with others. We will not blame our servant, neighbor, spouse or children as the cause of anything bad that happens to us.

Epictetus, *Discourses* 1.11.36-37 (Chuck Chakrapani, *Stoic Foundations* Ch. 11)

The way things are

The cause of our unhappiness is the way we think about things: what happens in our life and how other people behave. We are not upset by the cup breaking. We implicitly believe that the cup "shouldn't break." It is this judgment that makes us upset. We are not angry at someone bumping into us. We are angry because we think that people should look where they are going. It is this judgment that causes us grief. We are not worried because of the traffic jam. We are upset because we think that we will be late, and this will cause us problems. It is these judgments that cause to worry.

What happened	Our judgment	Our reaction
Our favorite cup breaks	*The cup shouldn't break.*	We are upset
Someone bumps into us	*They should look up.*	We are angry
There's traffic jam	*It is a terrible thing.*	We are worried

It is not the external things that cause our unhappiness, but the way we think about them—our judgment. We have trained ourselves so well into thinking that external things are the cause of our problems that we don't stop to think that they have nothing to do with our problems. The way we think about them is the problem. If we train ourselves to think differently, we will act differently, and we will feel differently. Imagine the following situations.

1. *You have just spotted a parking spot and you are about to back into it. As you are about to back in, a car behind you moves into that spot. You believe that the other person knows that you were there before him and yet he moved into that spot anyway. He gets out of his car with a smirk on his face.*

How do you feel about that? Now imagine this:

2. *You have just spotted a parking spot and you are about to back into it. As you are about to back in, a car behind you moves into that spot. You believe that the other person knows that you were there before him and yet he moved into that spot anyway. As the other driver is parking, you notice that the spot was reserved for disabled people and a person with a limp gets out of the other car.*

How do you feel now?

If you are like most people, you would be angry in the first scenario and probably a bit embarrassed in the second for trying to steal a disabled spot. But in both scenarios the external events that affect you are identical:

- You thought you had a parking spot.
- Someone else took it away in the last minute.
- You must find another spot.

Even though the external events that affect you are identical, in one scenario your judgment was that what happened was unfair and in the other scenario your judgment was that what happened was fair. It is your judgment that made you angry or ashamed. Not the external event itself.

It is so in every case. It doesn't matter whether the problem is small or big. Suppose two people lose their job. The first person may believe that it is a good thing because she always wanted to look for a better job but was too lazy to do it. She sees this as an opportunity because it will force her to look for a better job. Her judgment makes the job loss a positive thing. The second person might believe it is a terrible thing because now he must look for another job and he would rather not. It is not the job loss but the judgment about job loss that made one person happy and another unhappy. If we analyze any life situation, we will realize that it is not the external things but our judgments about them that cause our problems.

What about things that most people consider terrible—things such as death, poverty, and physical harm?

- *People fear death.* Yet a soldier faces death willingly.
- *People fear poverty.* Yet parents voluntarily deprive themselves of many things for the welfare of their children.
- *People are afraid of physical harm.* Yet a mother jumps in front of an oncoming vehicle to save her child, knowing she could be harmed.

Clearly, even where things like death, poverty, or physical harm are involved, it is our judgment that makes us avoid them or not worry about them.

> If you are pained by anything external, the pain is not due to the external thing. It is due to the way you look at it.
>
> Marcus Aurelius, *Meditations*, 8.47 (Chuck Chakrapani, *Stoic Meditations*, Ch. 8)

Why is this important?

You may say, "OK, I understand, but so what? I am still justified in my reaction. Why shouldn't I be angry when someone steals my parking spot? How can I not be depressed when I have lost my job?" The simple answer is if your problems are caused by your judgments rather than by what happened, you can learn to judge things differently. You will have no fear of dying if you believe death is not a bad thing. You will not be afraid of poverty if you don't think poverty is a bad thing. Otherwise, every time something that is not to your liking happens, you are going to be unhappy.

Of course, it is easier said than done. It is one thing to understand that our judgments cause our unhappiness, but quite another to be tranquil when something "bad" happens to us. The purpose of this course is to supply the foundation for you to *move towards* happiness, freedom, and tranquility step by step. Let's start slowly and with a simple exercise that you will do throughout this week at any time you feel angry, upset, worried, or fearful. The purpose of this exercise (and the ones that follow) is to build your Stoic muscles, slowly and painlessly. In the coming weeks, we will see how to make the right judgments that will lead us to a happy life.

> Nothing important comes into being overnight... Be patient.
>
> Epictetus, *Discourses* 1.15.7 (Chuck Chakrapani, *Stoic Foundations*, Ch. 15)

Key takeaways

1. *Our happiness is not the result of what happens to us.*
2. *Our happiness is the result of what we think is happening to us.*
3. *To be happy we need to judge everything that is presented to us in the right way.*

Selected readings. Week 2

1. It is your judgments that disturb you

[FROM Epictetus, *Enchiridion*, 5, Chuck Chakrapani, *The Good Life Handbook*, Ch. 5]

Events don't disturb people, the way they think about events does. Even death is not frightening by itself. But our view of death, that it is something we should be afraid of, frightens us.

So, when we are frustrated, angry, or unhappy, let's hold ourselves responsible for these emotions because they are the result of our judgments. No one else is responsible for them.

When you blame others for your negative feelings, you are being ignorant. When you blame yourself for your negative feelings, you are making progress. You are being wise when you stop blaming yourself or others.

2 It is your judgments that scare you

[FROM Epictetus, *Discourses*, 2.16, Chuck Chakrapani, *Stoic Choices*. Ch.16]

We are spirited, fluent, and ready to answer classroom questions and draw the right conclusion. In real life, though, we are miserably lost at sea. Let a disturbing thought arise, then we will see what we really practiced and trained for. Because we don't practice, we keep piling up worries, believing that our problems are worse than they are.

For example, when I am on a cruise, I look around and see nothing but water. I am gripped by fear. What if I drown? I have to drink all this sea. It doesn't occur to me that swallowing just three pints of water will do me in. Is it the sea that scares me? No, it is my own judgment that scares me. Or, consider the earthquake. I imagine that the whole city is going to fall on me, even though a little brick will knock my brain out.

"So, what weighs us down and scares us?"

"Our own judgments, obviously."

"What scares you when you are about to leave your country—leaving friends, family, familiar places, and familiar people?"

"Again, our own judgments."

"Children cry when the nanny leaves. Give them a cake and the nanny is forgotten."

"Are you asking us to model ourselves after children?"

"Of course not. You don't need a cake, but correct judgments."

---

3. Everything has two handles

[FROM: Epictetus, *Enchiridion*, 43, Chuck Chakrapani, *The Good Life Handbook,* Ch. 43]

Everything has two handles, the one by which it may be carried, the other by which it cannot. If your brother acts unjustly, don't lay hold on the action by the handle of his injustice for by that it cannot be carried; but by the opposite, that he is your brother, that he was brought up with you; and thus you will lay hold on it, as it is to be carried."

Exercise 2. The Two Handles

When to use it

Use the Two Handles technique whenever you are upset by the actions of other people or things that happen that are not to your liking.

The main purpose of the Two Handles technique is to make you aware that it is your judgment that created your unhappiness. You can change your judgment to the one that will lead you to happiness.

How does it work

You can judge any situation in two ways—one that leads to unhappiness and the other, to happiness. When you are unhappy with something, you have made a wrong judgment; it is incompatible with happiness. You picked it up by the wrong handle. Choose the other handle that will lead you to happiness, by grabbing the other handle. For example,

Suppose your friend did something to hurt you.

You are angry and unhappy because you are using the handle, "My friend hurt me." This makes you angry and unhappy. So, this handle is the wrong one.

Ask yourself "what other handle can I use here?" The other handle could be, "We all do thoughtless things from time to time. I'm sure I have hurt others as well. I don't have to take it that seriously. He is a friend and it is no big deal." This handle is compatible with happiness. So, it is the right handle. Our friend's behavior no longer hurts us.

When you are upset with your boss, the handle, "He is a jerk," or, "He doesn't appreciate me," or, "He doesn't know what he is talking about," or, 'He is being unreasonable," is the incorrect handle. The handle, "I am grateful I have this job. Let me see why my boss is asking me to do this. Let me understand this from their perspective," or "My boss may be wrong, but so am I at times. Why make a big deal of it?" is likely to diffuse anger and likely to lead to a more pleasant interaction with your boss.

Additional comments

Do this exercise as many times as possible during the day. When you go to bed, review your day. If you did this exercise less than three times during the day, it could be that you failed to notice your discomfort in different situations. Mentally go over the day, looking for times when you were irritated, annoyed, angry, anxious, or worried—even mildly. Then ask yourself what the judgment was that led you to your discomfort. Think about "the other handle" that would have relieved your discomfort.

Daily quotes. Week 2

Sunday

[Things] ... are what they are ... and they don't pass any judgment upon themselves. What judges them, then? Your reasoning mind.

M. Aurelius, *Meditations*, 9.42 (Chuck Chakrapani, *Stoic Meditations*, 9.42)

Monday

A happy person is one who can make a right judgment in all things: happy with one's present circumstances, whatever they may be; satisfied and on friendly terms with the conditions of life. That person is happy whose reason guides all their activities.

Seneca, *On the Happy* Life, 6, (Chuck Chakrapani, *Stoic Happiness*, Ch. 6)

Tuesday

Throw away your [negative] judgments and you are saved. Who is stopping you from doing this?

M. Aurelius, *Meditations*, 12.25 (Chuck Chakrapani, *Stoic Meditations*, 12.25)

Wednesday

Nothing but your own judgment is capable of causing us to become disturbed and confused.

Epictetus, *Discourses* 3.19.3 (Chuck Chakrapani, *Stoic Training*, Ch. 11)

Thursday

What, after all, is sighing and crying, except opinions? What is misfortune? An opinion.

Epictetus, *Discourses* 3.3.18 (Chuck Chakrapani, *Stoic Training*, Ch. 3)

Friday

When someone provokes you, if you respond with anger or some other negative emotion, your mind is tricked into believing you are being harmed ... Take some time before reacting. You will see you are in better control.

Epictetus, *Enchiridion*, 20 (Chuck Chakrapani, *The Good Life Handbook*, Ch.10)

Saturday

For it is not the hardship or death that is a fearful thing, but the fear of hardship or death.

Epictetus, *Discourses* 2.1 (Chuck Chakrapani, *Stoic Choices*, Ch. 1)

Foundation 3. What We Can't Control is Nothing to Us

Lesson 3

Big idea 3. Don't worry about things you can't control

Most of the things that we worry about—such as our job security, what people think of us, illness, health, and accidents—are external to us. They are not under our control. Even though we seem to have some control over these things, ultimately, we don't control them. Worrying about things not under our control is meaningless and illogical because our worry, anger, and depression have no effect on outside events. We can increase the quality of our life dramatically if we stop worrying about things beyond our control.

So, there is only one sure way to happiness, tranquility, and freedom. It is to deal with the things that are under our control and stop worrying about what is not under our control. What we don't control is nothing to us.

There is only one way to be happy. Keep this thought ready for use morning, noon, and night. Give up the desire for things not under your control.

Epictetus, *Discourses* 4.4.39 (Chuck Chakrapani, *Stoic Freedom*, Ch. 4)

We don't control externals

We don't control external things. What do these "externals" include? They include many things that we normally think *are* under our control—such as our body, what we own now, what people think of us, and our job. This may sound strange to you. Take your body for example. You may feel it is under your control. When you exercise and eat right, your body is healthy. When you neglect your body, it weakens. So, you get the feeling that you control your body. But if you think more about it, you will realize that even if you exercise and eat right, you can fall ill. Even if you are healthy, eventually your body will grow old and die. Or your body could be damaged in an accident.

This is true of all other external things, whether it is reputation or your job or your relationship. No matter how solid they look to you now, eventually they are not under your control.

Because externals are not under our control, we should take them as they come. We don't need to label them as good and bad, or evil. We don't need to avoid them, and we don't need to seek them. We don't need to like them, and we don't need to hate them. They are just what they are. It's reality. No matter what the external conditions are, it is possible for us to build a happy life.

You have power over your mind—not outside events.
Realize this, and you will find strength.

Attributed to Marcus Aurelius

Don't become attached to external things

Externals by themselves cannot make us happy or unhappy. When we believe that they do and become attached to them, we sow the seeds of suffering. For example, it is perfectly alright to enjoy a glass of wine. But the moment you feel that you *must* have a glass of wine to fully enjoy your meal, you are becoming attached to it. Then, instead of enjoying wine when you have it, you are unhappy why you don't. Wine becomes your master and you the slave to it. The same is true whether the external is alcohol, food, relationship, reputation, health, or wealth. You can enjoy all these when you have them. But you don't need them to be happy. If they go, let them go.

Look around you in every direction. Mentally get rid of everything.

Keep your judgments pure. See that you become attached to nothing that doesn't belong to you and can be painful if taken away from you.

Epictetus, *Discourses* IV.1.112 (Chuck Chakrapani, *Stoic Freedom*, Ch.1)

Attachment to externals makes you a slave

If today is Sunday, there is no point wishing it were Tuesday. No matter how hard you wish, it is going to be Sunday. But we do not realize the same thing is true when we get sick or lose money in the stock market. No matter how hard we wish that we were not sick or had not lost money, nothing is going to change. We might as well get on with our lives. What we cannot control is nothing to us. Believing that somehow you control externals can harm you.

Worse still, becoming attached to externals makes us a slave of externals. It also makes us a slave for those who control the externals we desire. If you want your job to be 100% secure, you become the slave of the person who has the power to fire you. If you are attached to having a relationship with a person, you become a slave to the other person.

If you are after money, the person who controls it will become your master.

> Show me one who is not a slave. One is a slave to lust, another to greed, another to ambition, and all are slaves to fear.
>
> Seneca, *Moral Letters*, 47.17

Avoiding external things also makes you a slave

Aversion to an external is the flipside of attachment to it. When you desperately want to avoid something, it means that you don't like reality and you want it to go away. Reality doesn't care to cooperate with what you want. This results in unhappiness. If you hate crowds, you will be unhappy in crowded places. If you detest alcohol, you will be upset by people who drink. To be free, we need to take reality as it is. We should be neither carried away nor repulsed by it. Externals are the way they are, whether we like it or not. Externals don't care for our approval. But there is no reason to avoid externals. If it is desirable (such as our health or job), we enjoy it when it comes our way. If not, we don't miss it. We don't "hate" any external things.

> If we attach value to externals of any kind, it would make us submissive to others.
>
> Epictetus, *Discourse* 4.4. (Chuck Chakrapani, *Stoic Freedom*, Ch. 14)

Why we become attached to externals

We become attached to things because of our judgment that they are good or that they are bad. Suppose you have a beautiful painting by a master. If someone steals it, you are distressed *because* you judge it to be precious. How is that different from the reaction of children who take a worthless piece of seashell, consider it precious, and become distressed if it is taken away? When we don't consider an external thing so special that we get attached to it, we can enjoy it when we have it and yet not be distressed if we lose it.

Everything depends on our judgment. Why is an expensive designer dress better than a regular store-bought dress, if both do the function of a dress equally well and last equally long? Because we judge it to be so. As we look more closely, we realize the value of externals comes from our judgment. We are envious if someone earns more money for the same job we do because we judge money to be precious and to define our worth. If we don't think that way, then we don't care what others are paid. If some things look valuable to us, it is because we put those things on a pedestal. Take away that pedestal. It is not any taller.

It is the same when we view people who are famous as awe-inspiring, people with power as more important, and people with money as worthy of admiration. We make up these things in our minds and then act as though they are real.

> How contemptible are the things we admire—like children who regard every toy as a thing of value ... What then ... is the difference between us and them except that we elders go crazy over paintings and sculpture, making our folly more expensive?
>
> Seneca, *Moral Letters*, 115.8

Externals can neither help you nor harm you

Externals can harm us or hurt us only when we value them. When we value externals, we think they have the power to harm us or help us. If we don't believe that poverty is a horrible thing, then losing our money is nothing to us; when we believe that being wealthy is important to us, then we give poverty the power to make us unhappy. If we don't believe that death is a terrible thing, no one can threaten us with death; if we believe that death is a terrible thing, then we are afraid of anyone who has the power to take life away. If someone insults us, we are offended only because we believe that we should not be insulted; if you think it is just somebody else's opinion and it doesn't affect who you are, then it doesn't have to offend you.

Forget the belief "I've been harmed" and you won't feel harmed.

Reject the sense of injury and injury itself disappears.

Marcus Aurelius, *Meditations*, 4.7 (Chuck Chakrapani, *Stoic Meditations*, Ch. 4.7)

Key takeaways

1. *External things such as money, status, possessions, and relationships have no power to make us happy or unhappy.*
2. *But when we believe that they are important to our happiness, we give externals the power to hurt us or please us.*
3. *Just as children who believe worthless things are of value and cry if they are taken away, we believe external things are of value and are unhappy when they are taken away.*

Selected Readings

1. Avoid only things under your control

[FROM Epictetus, *Enchiridion*, 2; Chuck Chakrapani, *The Good Life Handbook*, Ch.2]

We are ruled by our desires and aversions. When we desire something, we aim to get it. If we don't get what we desire, we feel disappointed.

When we are averse to something, we want to avoid it. If we end up getting what we don't want anyway, we feel unhappy.

If you desire and avoid only those things that are under your control, then you will not feel victimized by things you dislike. But if you resent unavoidable things like illness, misfortune, or death, that are not under your control, you are headed for disappointment.

Instead of showing dislike for what you cannot control, direct your dislike to things that are under your control but are contrary to your nature.

For now, suspend your desires. If you desire something outside your control you are bound to be disappointed. Even when we do control things, the outcome may not be what we desire.

Select carefully what you want to choose and what you want to refuse. Be disciplined and detached while making the choice.

2. Choose not to go after external things

[FROM Epictetus, *Discourses* 2.2; Chuck Chakrapani. *Stoic Choices*, Ch. 2]

The following is a discourse by Epictetus. He asks us not to go after externals. He also says that, just because we don't care for externals, we should not provoke others unnecessarily either. In particular, he makes the following points.

1. *When you are the master of your desires and emotions, you win.*
2. *Going after externals makes you a slave.*
3. *Do not provoke others unnecessarily.*

You win when you control your desires and aversions

If you are going to court, consider what you want to keep and what you want to win. If your choice is fully in line with nature, you are totally secure. All will go as planned and you have nothing to worry about. When you guard what is your own, what is by nature free and want only those things, you need not worry about anything. No one else is the master, and no one else can take these things away from you. If you want to be a person of honor and trust, who can stop you? If you don't want to be stopped or forced to do something against your will, who is going to make you do it? The judge may pass a sentence which she may think is fearful. But how can she force you to react to it as being terrible? So long as you control your desires and aversions, there is nothing to worry about. This is your opening statement, your case, and your proof. This is your last word and your acquittal. This is why, when someone asked Socrates to prepare for the trial, he said

"Don't you think I have been preparing for this my entire life?"

"Preparing for it how?"

"I have minded my own business, never did anything wrong, either in public or in private."

Going after externals makes you a slave

However, if you want to preserve the externals such as your body, property, and reputation, that's a different story. Begin right now. Make every possible preparation. Study the character of the judge and your antagonist. If you must clasp men's knees, clasp them; if you must weep, weep; if you must groan, groan. When you go after externals you become a slave. Stop being pulled in different directions, wanting to be a slave at one time and wanting to be free at other times. Be one or the other fully: free or a slave, cultivated or ignorant, a fighting cock or a docile one. Endure being beaten to death or give in all at once. You don't want to be the person who withstands many blows and then gives in.

Do not provoke, except by intention

If Socrates wanted to preserve externals he would he have said, "Anytus and Meletus can kill me but not harm me"? Was he so foolish as not to see this path did not lead to that end, but elsewhere? Why then did he not only disregard the judges, but provoke them as well? Consider what my friend Heraclitus did in a trivial lawsuit about a piece of land in Rhodes. After proving his case, he went on to comment, "I don't care what your decision is going to be. I am not on trial, but you are." Thus, he lost his case. What need was there for this? Don't make any additional comments or even say that you are not going to make any additional comments, unless you want to provoke the judges deliberately, as Socrates did. If you are going to do that, why rise to speak? Why even answer the summons? If you want to be crucified, just wait. The cross will come. But if reason dictates that you should answer the summons and convince the judge to the best of your abilities, you must do so accordingly, while always maintaining your true character.

There is a price to pay for externals

Looked at this way, it is also ridiculous to say, "Give me some advice." What advice can I give you? You should rather say, "Enable my mind to adapt to whatever happens." To ask for some advice is like asking what name you should write when you are about to write a name. Suppose I say, "Dio", and your teacher comes along and says, "Theo," what will you write? If you have practiced writing, you know what to write no matter what is dictated to you. If you have not, what can I tell you? If conditions suggest something else, what will you say? What will you do? Remember this general principle and you will need no advice: if you go after externals you will be tossed up and down according to the will of the master. And who is your master? Anyone who has control over what you desire or what you want to avoid.

3. Take things as they come

[FROM Epictetus, *Discourses* 2.2; Chuck Chakrapani. *Stoic Choices*, Ch 2]

Don't complain

Remember this. The more value you attach to external things, the less free you are to choose. Things outside our control include not only office but freedom from office also; not only business but leisure also.

"Should I then spend my life in this chaos among the mob?"

"What do you mean by chaos? Among the mob? What's hard about that? Imagine you are at the Olympics. Regard the chaos as a festival. There too, one man shouts this, another man that. One pushes the other. Even in swimming pools there are many people. Yet, who doesn't enjoy the Olympics and feel sorry to leave?

Don't be hard to please. Don't complain about trivial things. "The vinegar is bad, it's sharp; the honey is foul, it upsets my stomach; I don't like the vegetables." Similarly, people say, "I don't like leisure, it's lonely; I don't like a crowd, it is noisy." If you happen to find yourself alone or with a few other people, call this peace and go along for the duration. Talk to yourself, work on your impressions, and sharpen your preconceptions. But, if you happen to find yourself in a crowd, call it the games, a festival, or a celebration. Try to share the festival with the world. What is more pleasing to a lover of humankind than the sight of many people? We take pleasure in seeing herds of cows and horses. We take delight in watching a fleet of ships. Why, then, hate the sight of a group of humans?

"But they are loud. I'll go deaf."

"All right. You go deaf. What's it to you? Will it stop you from judging impressions correctly? Who can stop you from using desire and aversion, choice and refusal according to nature? No noise, no shouting is loud enough to do that."

If you want peace, don't be a slave to desires

Why, then, are you upset? No public contest is without commotion. There must be trainers, supporters who cheer, many official supervisors, and many spectators.

"But I want to live in peace."

"Well then, mope and be miserable. That is what you deserve. What greater punishment do you deserve for ignoring and challenging God's will than to be miserable, dissatisfied, and envious? Don't you want to free yourself from all this?"

"Yes, but how can I do that?"

"You have heard often that you must get rid of your desires completely and be averse only to things that are within your power. You must give up all external things—body, reputation, fame, books, applause, office and freedom from office. Because desiring any of these things immediately makes you a slave, you are a subject, you can be restrained and compelled, and you are entirely at the control of others. Keep this verse by Cleanthes handy:

"Lead me, Zeus; lead me, Destiny."

Take things as they come

Do I have to go to Rome? I go to Rome. To Gyara? I go to Gyara. To Athens? I go to Athens. To prison? I go to prison. But if you say, "When do we get to Athens?" you are lost. If you don't get to Athens, you will be disappointed because your desire is not fulfilled. If you do get to Athens, you will be overjoyed for the wrong reasons. Again, if you are stopped from getting what you want, you are stuck with what you don't want. Therefore, forget these things.

"But Athens is beautiful."

"But happiness is much more beautiful; and having a peaceful and undisturbed mind, dependent on only yourself."

"But Rome is so crowded and noisy."

"But serenity is worth all these aggravations. It is the proper time. Let go of all your dislikes. Why are you like a donkey enduring the burden? Otherwise, you will always be slave to someone who can have you released or block your way. You will have to serve him as you would a devil."

There is only one way to be happy. Keep this thought ready for use morning, noon, and night. Give up the desire for things not under your control. Don't think of anything as your own. Hand over everything to fortune and the deity. Leave these things in the care of supervisors appointed by God. Meanwhile, you concern yourself with only one thing: what is your own and what is free from restrictions. When you read, read about this. Write about this. Listen about this.

Be happy with the present

Knowing all this, be happy for what you have. Be satisfied with what each moment brings. If any of these things you studied and learned prove useful to you in your actions, be joyful. If you have got rid of or reduced your tendency to impulsiveness, indecent language, recklessness, laziness, and if you are not motivated by the same things that motivated you once, at least not to the same extent, then every day becomes a festival: today because you acted well yesterday, tomorrow because you acted well today.

How much better reason is this for thanksgiving than a consulship or a governorship. These things come to you from your own self and from God. Remember who gave them, to whom, and why. If you are brought up to reason like this, how can you ever ask where you will be happy and where you will please God? No matter where they are, aren't people equally distant from God? And, no matter where they are, don't they all see the same thing?

Exercise 3: Externals Eliminator

When to use it

The purpose of this exercise is to become aware of things that are not in our control, things we cannot do anything about. Worrying about them, becoming angry about them, and wishing that reality were different is a meaningless waste of time and energy. It just makes us unhappy without solving the problem. Use this exercise to become conscious of your irrational belief that somehow you can affect reality that is not under your control by simply worrying about it or wishing it were different.

How it works

Feelings like worry, anger, and irritation arise within us a number of times in a day. It may not be serious. Yet it causes us discomfort. Consider situations like these:

- Your alarm didn't go off. You woke up 30 minutes late. Now you are worried you are going to be late to your morning meeting.
- Your friend told you that so-and-so is speaking ill of you behind your back. You are angry.
- You just found out that someone at work who is fairly incompetent is given a raise that is bigger than yours.
- You are told that you are in the early stages of cancer. It is curable, but it will cost you your life's savings.

Most of us go through some of these situations several times a day. We get mildly annoyed, irritated, or worried, but we do it so frequently that we fail even to notice it. These reactions create a general sense of uneasiness which prevents us from being happy. This week, let's become aware of our normal reactions to unwelcome things in our lives.

Whenever any situation creates anxiety, anger or worry in you, ask a single question.

Is this under my control?

If the answer is NO, it's nothing to you.

If the answer is YES, then also you don't have a problem. It is under your control, so fix it.

If your answer is PARTLY, set it aside for now. We will deal with it next week.

Most things that we normally worry about belong to the first category. We can't control them. They are nothing to us. Look at the first example above where your alarm didn't go off.

Is this under your control?

You may be tempted to say yes because it was you who forgot set the alarm, and so it was under your control. But the key point is that it *was* under your control. You can't go back and change the past. So, it is *now* not under your control. If you are going to be late, you are going to be late. Worrying about it will not change the situation. So, it is nothing to you. You might as well relax.

That's all you need to do for this week. Practice this every day at every opportunity.

Additional comments

Do this exercise any time you feel uncomfortable, angry, or worried about a situation. For most of us, this can be several times a day. During this week, do this exercise every day as often as possible. *At a bare minimum* do it at least three times a day. If you did it less than three times in a day, you probably failed to notice your feelings through the day. So, at night, mentally go through the day looking for times when you were irritated, annoyed, angry, anxious, worried—even mildly. Then ask yourself the two questions for each such situation you identify.

Quotes for week 3

Sunday

There is only one road to happiness ... stay detached from things that are not up to you.

Epictetus, *Discourses* 3.3.39 (Chuck Chakrapani, *Stoic Training*, Ch. 3)

Monday

If you gape after externals, you must of necessity ramble up and down, in obedience to the will of your master. And who is your master? He who has the power over the things which you seek to gain or avoid.

Epictetus *Discourses* 2.2.25-26; Chuck Chakrapani. *Stoic Choices*, Ch. 2)

Tuesday

Stop being pulled in different directions, wanting to be a slave at one time and wanting to be free at other times. Be one or the other fully: free or a slave, cultivated or ignorant, a fighting cock or a docile one. Endure being beaten to death or give in all at once. You don't want to be the person who withstands many blows and then gives in.

Epictetus *Discourses* 2.2: (Chuck Chakrapani. *Stoic Choices*, Ch. 2)

Wednesday

The more value you attach to external things the less free you are to choose.

Epictetus, *Discourses* Bk 4.4; (Chuck Chakrapani. *Stoic Freedom*, Ch. 4)

Thursday

Don't complain about trivial things: "The vinegar is bad, it's sharp;" "the honey's foul, it upsets my stomach;" "I don't like the vegetables."

Epictetus, *Discourses* Bk 4.4; (Chuck Chakrapani, *Stoic Freedom*, Ch. 4)

Friday

The purpose of studying is to get rid of complaints, misfortunes, disappointments, and self-pity.

Epictetus, *Discourses* Bk 1.4; (Chuck Chakrapani. *Stoic Foundations*, Ch. 4)

Saturday

What are tragic stories except descriptions of people who went after external things that were not under their control, failed, and as a result, suffered?

Epictetus, *Discourses* Bk 1.4; (Chuck Chakrapani. *Stoic Foundations*, Ch. 4)

Foundation 4. Act on What You Control

Lesson 4

Big idea 4. Act on what you can control

Ignoring what is beyond our control can end a lot of our problems. However, to have a truly flourishing life we need to go a step further: We also need to act on what is within our control.

Winning a game may not be under your control. But playing the game well and enjoying it *is* under your control.

Whether you will keep your job or lose it may not be under your control. But doing your job well so you are less likely to lose it *is* under your control.

Eradicating poverty in the world may not be under your control. But helping someone who is poor *is* under your control.

In fact, when we concentrate only on what we do control, we increase the chance of avoiding undesirable outcomes.

If you deal with only those things that are under your control, no one can force you to do anything you don't want to do; no one can stop you.

You will have no enemy and no harm will come to you.

Epictetus *Enchiridion*, 5 (Chuck Chakrapani, *The Good Life Handbook*, Ch.5)

Acting on what you control

Acting on what is within your power is one of the most neglected aspects of Stoic philosophy. People who look at Stoicism superficially often believe that Stoicism simply tells us to accept whatever life presents to us and therefore it is a philosophy of inaction and passivity. Therefore, they argue, Stoics do nothing to better themselves or society. This is far from the truth. Historically, Stoics were people of action, unafraid and active. While they didn't act on what was not under their control, they certainly acted on what *was* under their control.

Let any difficulty come my way. I have the resources and constitution ... to deal with whatever happens.

Epictetus *Discourses* 1.6; (Chuck Chakrapani. *Stoic Foundations*, Ch. 6)

What exactly do we control?

We control
- What we think.
- How we think.
- What we desire.
- What we avoid.
- How we choose to act.
- How we chose not to act.

In short, we are in total control of what comes from us: what we think, desire, and do. If it doesn't come from us, we don't control it, even if we are convinced that we do. For example, whether you will win a competition or not is not under your control, even if you think it is. But training hard to increase your chances of winning is under your control. Whether society will change in a positive way or not is not under your control. But taking proper actions that will increase the probability that society will change is under your control.

Even so, you realize that winning a competition and changing society to a more positive state are not under your control. So, you accept whatever the outcome is. But training to win and taking actions that will help society are under your control. So, you act. Stoicism teaches us to ignore completely what is not under our control. It also teaches us to concentrate totally on what is under our control. The second part—acting on things under your control—is as important for the good life as the first part—ignoring what is not under your control.

Life is indifferent. But the way we use it is not indifferent.

Epictetus *Discourses* 2.6.1; (Chuck Chakrapani, *Stoic Choices*, Ch. 6)

Recognize that you control your reactions

One of our biggest mistakes in thinking is to believe that what is not under our control *is* in our control, and that what is under control *is not* our control. If we observe conversations, you will often find people saying things that imply what is under their control is not under their control.

- *It is not my fault. He started it.*

You cannot control what someone else starts. But whether you want to carry on along the same lines is your choice.

- *She made me do it.*

What someone else does is not under your control. But they cannot make you do anything. That is your choice.

- *Given what happened, I have a right to be angry.*

Given what happened you may have the "right" to be angry. But being angry is your choice.

- *How do you expect me to enjoy my dinner, when I just lost my job?*

Not enjoying your dinner will not bring your job back. You are adding to your problems. I don't "expect" you to enjoy your dinner, but whether you want to enjoy it or not is your choice.

Now, if we have trained ourselves to believe (with a lot of social support) that our behavior is determined by 'other people or some external circumstance, it is not going to be easy to believe that we are the cause of our unhappiness. The exercises in this course are designed to retrain your mind and help you see things as they are.

> Our job is to make careful and skillful use of the [dice] that have fallen, even though we don't know what is going to fall.
>
> Epictetus *Discourses* Bk 2.5.3; (Chuck Chakrapani. *Stoic Choices*, Ch. 5)

Act on what you can control

Many things in life are not under our control. In fact, no external thing is really under our control. And yet, we can influence many external things by our actions. Our actions are under our control. When this is the case, we act on that part over which we have control.

In many situations, while the result may not be under our control, many actions that may influence the outcome are under our control. So, whenever we face a situation that is not under our control, we look for things that *are* under our control and act on them.

You got fired

Your boss just told you that your services are no longer needed.

That's not under your control. What your boss says comes from her, not from you. So, it is nothing to you.

What is under your control?

Things like these are under your control: Enjoying your meal or going for walk after losing your job; getting in touch with your friends and acquaintances to see if they are aware of any opportunities for you; contacting a recruiter; searching social media for job announcements.

Looking for and doing things under your control is far more productive than feeling sorry for yourself and blaming others for your job loss. These actions are under your control and you can do them instead of brooding over your job loss.

A hurricane

A hurricane is heading toward a Caribbean island where you have planned (and paid for) a long-awaited vacation.

That's not under your control. So, there is no point in worrying about it. It is nothing to you.

What is under your control?

Once you understand the impact of the storm on your destination, you can explore whether your trip is still possible. If it is not, you can do what you can to be reimbursed. You can start to plan a different trip. If you are able, you can donate to the country's relief fund. All these things are under your control.

Missing your flight

You are driving to catch a flight. There is a big accident and two lanes are closed. You are almost certain to miss the flight.

This is not under your control. You didn't create the traffic and you cannot stop it. You may miss the flight.

What is under your control?

To relax, enjoy the music. This is under your control. Realize that being tense has no effect on whether you are going to catch your flight or not. By worrying about it, you are only wasting your time. You might as well enjoy the music.

If you deal with only those things under your control, no one can force you to do what you don't want to do. No one can stop you.

You will have no enemies and no harm will come to you.

Epictetus *Enchiridion* 1 (Chuck Chakrapani, *The Good Life Handbook*, Ch. 1)

Key takeaways

1. *Acting on what we have control over is as important as ignoring what we don't have control over.*

2. *While external things are not under our control, acting in a way that would make a desired outcome more likely may be in our control.*

3. *In every external circumstance that is presented to us we need to ask, "Is there anything under my control that I can do which is likely to lead to (but not guarantee) a desirable outcome"?* Act on the part that is under your control, without expecting that you will reach the desired outcome.

Selected Readings

1. Enjoy every sandwich

[FROM Chuck Chakrapani, *Unshakable Freedom*, Ch.3]

How do you attain unshakable freedom? By controlling what is under your control. A sailor does not control the wind. Complaining about the wind does not make the wind go away, but it makes the sailor miserable and ineffective. By trying to control the wind, the sailor fails to control the sails. No matter how bad the wind, you can control only the sails.

This is so about everything we face. You can only control what is under your control. Either something is under our control or it is not. If we are to be sure of achieving freedom, by definition, it should come from what is under our control. We are not free because we fail to make this most basic distinction.

What is not in your control is neither good nor bad. It is just the way it is; it is reality. You cannot reject reality without feeling trapped. Whatever you choose to think about reality, it is not under your control. When it rains, you cannot stop it. But if you don't want to get wet, you can carry an umbrella. If your thinking is "in accordance with nature" you cannot be hindered by anyone. You are free, and you will blame no one.

Why is this being "in accordance with nature" so important? Simply because nature, gives us no other option. There is no point in arguing with reality. Reality has a track record of winning every time. No exceptions.

But living according to nature has also provided us with a weapon to counter the "negative" effects of reality on us. It is our ability to think rationally and to choose our thoughts. This simple principle is the basis of unshakable freedom.

But can we still be free when so many things are not under our control? Yes, say the Stoics.

How?

By controlling the things that are under our control.

Here you are, stuck in traffic. You are already late. You did not create the traffic. Even if you are in some way responsible for being there at that time, you are already in it.

So, the traffic jam is a given. It is there as part of your current reality. You have only two choices. You can go through the imagined consequences of your being late in your mind repeatedly and feel miserable. You can blame public works, the accident, drivers who don't know how to drive, the weather, or whatever you think caused the delay, and feel agitated. Or, you can consider this a gift of time to you and use it to listen to music, plan your day, or simply relax.

Either way, the traffic is going to be there, and you are going to be late. Your being imprisoned by negative thoughts and anger is not decided by the traffic, but by what you choose to think.

Death, be not proud

You can make this idea work whether the situation is trivial, like being stuck in traffic, or serious, like having cancer and a prognosis of only a few months to live.

That was exactly what happened to the musician Warren William Zevon. In the year 2000, he released a prophetically titled album, *Life'll Kill Ya*, containing the song "Don't Let Us Get Sick." Well, your health is not under your control. Shortly before playing at the Edmonton Folk Festival in 2002, he started feeling dizzy, developed a chronic cough, and was diagnosed with mesothelioma.

What were his choices? He could have felt sorry for himself and spent his remaining days in fear. Instead, he began recording his final album, *The Wind*, and invited his friends Bruce Springsteen, Don Henley, Jackson Browne, Timothy B. Schmidt, Joe Walsh, David Lindley, Billy Bob Thornton, Emmylou Harris, Tom Petty, Dwight Yoakam, and others to participate. He continued to maintain his caustic sense of humor, even as his health kept deteriorating.

Later the same year, Warren Zevon appeared on the Late Show with David Letterman. Letterman asked him what he had learned in the process of dying. Zevon replied, "I learned to enjoy every sandwich."

Zevon was told that his illness was terminal, but he continued to live as well as he could. Months after his diagnosis, he saw the birth of twin grandsons in June 2003 and the release of *The Wind* on August 26, 2003. He died two weeks later.

Among other things, Warren Zevon's declaration, "enjoy every sandwich," inspired Lee Lipsenthal, a California physician dying of cancer in 2011, when he was facing his own mortality. Lee described his journey from the diagnosis up to his eventual passing and published it under the title, *Enjoy Every Sandwich*. Lipsenthal wrote, "Pay attention to the good stuff that happens every day and enjoy what is, not what should have been or what might be. Enjoy every sandwich. My life is a sandwich, and I might as well savor every bite."

Epictetus said, "There is only one way to happiness and that is to cease worrying about things which are beyond the power of our will." (Epictetus, *Discourses*, 4.4.39) Zevon's terminal illness was beyond his will. But his decisions to enjoy every sandwich and put together a final album with his friends were not. By choosing to enjoy every sandwich over enduring several fearful final months, he died free of fear. This is unshakable freedom. It is open to us all.

2. Externals are not in our power. Our choice is.

[FROM Epictetus *Discourses* 2.5; Chuck Chakrapani *Stoic Choices*, Ch.5]

We can be obstructed only in matters we don't control

Where something is not indifferent, no one can obstruct and compel us. We can be obstructed or compelled only in matters over which we have no control. These are neither good nor bad, because they are not based on our choices. Blending the two—the carefulness of one devoted to material things with the stability of one who disregards them—may appear difficult, but it is not impossible. In fact, it is essential for our happiness.

Do what is in your control and deal with the rest as it unfolds

Say you are going on a voyage. What can you do? Whatever is in your power: Pick the captain, the ship, the day, and the time. Then a storm rises. It's no longer your business, it's the captain's. You have done everything you could. Now the ship starts to sink. What can you do now? The only thing you can do—sink. But without fear, without crying, and without accusing God; as one who knows what is born must also die. You are not eternal, but a human being. A part of the whole, as an hour is of the day. An hour ends. So does your life. What difference is there in dying whether it be by drowning or by fever? You must die one way or another.

This is what skillful ballplayers do. They don't consider the ball good or bad but only how to throw it and how to catch it. Grace, skill, speed, and expertise lie in that. While I can't catch their throws even if I spread my coat to do it, they can catch the ball wherever I throw it. But if we are nervous about throwing or catching the ball, there's no fun in it. How can we keep ourselves steady and see what comes next?

"Throw it," says one; "Don't throw it," says another; "You have thrown it already once," says yet another. It would become more a quarrel than a game.

In this sense, Socrates was a ballplayer. He played in the courtroom. He challenged, "Tell me, Anytus, how can you say I don't believe in God? Who do you think are the daemons? Have we not agreed that they are offspring of gods or of gods and humans?"

Anytus agreed.

"Tell me, then," Socrates continued, "If someone accepts that there are mules, shouldn't they also accept there are horses and donkeys, the animals that produced them?"

Clearly, Socrates was playing ball. The ball in this case was his life, prison, exile, or execution; being separated from his wife and his children becoming orphans. These were the stakes and yet he played—with skill.

Be careful *how* you play ball, but be indifferent to the ball itself

We need to play the same way: Careful about *how* we play, while being indifferent to the ball itself. We need to show skill in dealing with external materials, without becoming attached them. A weaver does not make the wool but uses her skills on the wool she is given. Whoever has given you food and property can take them back, and your body too. Accept what you are given and work on it.

If you come off unharmed, people who meet you will congratulate you on your escape. But an insightful person will praise you and share your pleasure only if you have acted honorably. He will do the opposite if you have gained your success through dishonest means. When a person has a proper reason to celebrate, others have a reason to join in the celebration.

3. On understanding the importance of action

[FROM: Epictetus, *Discourses*, 2.9; Chuck Chakrapani, *Stoic Choices*, Ch. 9]

Key ideas of this discourse

1. *Each person or thing is strengthened and preserved by actions that reflect its nature: Modesty is preserved by modest actions, and trustworthiness is preserved by trustworthy behavior.*
2. *Each person or thing is weakened and destroyed by actions that are contrary to its nature: Modesty is destroyed by shamelessness, and trustworthiness is destroyed by untrustworthy behavior.*
3. *Over time, we start behaving in a way that is contrary to what we learnt.*
4. *We are quick to recite the principles of Stoicism but don't live by them.*
5. *This is because we are trying to be a philosopher when we can barely fulfill the role of a human being.*

How human beings are preserved and destroyed

It is not easy to fulfill our role as human beings.

"What is a human being?"

"A rational, mortal animal."

"What does our rational nature distinguish us from?"

"From wild animals and animals like sheep."

"Then take care not to act like sheep and thus destroy your humanity. When we act to satisfy our gluttony and sexual desires, when our actions are random, dirty, and thoughtless, to what level have we sunk?"

"To that of wild beasts."

Some of us are large wild beasts. Others are small animals, little evil-natured creatures, which make us say, "I would rather be eaten by a lion."

All such actions destroy our calling as human beings.

A complex thing is preserved when it fulfils its functions and when different parts of a complex thing are true. A discrete thing is preserved when it fulfils its function. When are flutes, a lyre, a horse, a dog preserved? Why then, are we to be surprised if humans are preserved the same way and destroyed the same way?

Everything is strengthened and preserved by actions that reflect its nature

Each person is strengthened and preserved by actions that reflect his nature: A carpenter by the art of carpentry, a grammar expert by grammatical studies. If the grammar expert starts writing ungrammatically, his art will be destroyed. Modesty is preserved by modest actions but destroyed by shameless ones; trustworthiness is preserved by trustworthy behavior while behavior contrary to it destroys it.

Acts of opposite character preserve the opposite character: shamelessness by shameless behavior, dishonesty by dishonest behavior, viciousness by vice, a bad temper by anger, and miserliness by disproportionate taking as opposed to giving.

This is why we shouldn't be content just to learn, but must add practice, followed by training. Over time, we get into the habit of doing the opposite of what we learn and use opinions that are the opposite of correct ones. So, unless we apply the correct opinions, we will just be interpreting other people's judgments.

Anyone can talk the talk

We can all talk the talk: What is good and evil? Some things are good, some evil, and others indifferent. Virtues and things related to them are good. Evil is the opposite. Indifferents are things like health, wealth, and reputation. Then we are interrupted. There is a loud noise. Someone laughs at us. We are immediately upset. Tell me, philosopher, what happened to the things you were just talking about? Where was it coming from? Your lips. That's all. Then, why do you pervert helpful thoughts that are not yours? Why do you gamble with important things?

Can you walk the walk?

Storing wine and bread in your pantry is one thing, eating them is another. What you eat is digested and distributed around your body and it becomes sinews, flesh, bones, blood, a good complexion, and easy breathing. What is stored away is ready and available for display whenever you choose. But you get no benefit from it, except a reputation for owning it.

So, what difference does it make whether you talk about the teachings of this school or some other school? Maybe you will give a better account of the teachings of Epicurus than Epicurus himself! Why call yourself a Stoic and deceive others? Why act the part of a Jew when you are a Greek? Don't you know the reason a person is called a Jew, a Syrian or an Egyptian? When someone wavers between two faiths, we say, "He is no Jew. He is just acting the part." But once he makes his choice and assumes the attitude of one who is baptized, he is really a Jew and we call him one. So also, we are fake Baptists; Jews in name only, but something quite different. We do not follow our principles but are proud we know them.

Don't try to be a philosopher when you can barely be a human being

We take on the role of a philosopher when we can barely fulfill the role of a human being, even though it is a massive burden. It is like a person who can't lift ten pounds wanting to lift the rock of Ajax!

Think about this

Modest acts preserve the modest man, whereas immodest acts destroy him; and faithful acts preserve the faithful man while acts of the opposite character destroy him.

Epictetus, *Discourses* 2.9 (Chuck Chakrapani, *Stoic Choices*, Ch. 9)

Exercise 4. Action Activator

When to use it

As we saw in the previous lesson, many things are not under our control. And yet, even in such situations, we can choose to act in a way that increases our effectiveness and leads to happiness. The outcome may not be under our control, but still many actions that might influence the outcome may be under our control. Often, we fail to notice what is under our control because we are too preoccupied with our frustration about what is beyond our control. This technique is helpful in identifying what is under our control and how to act on it.

Do this exercise any time you feel you are frustrated with a situation. It could be your boss being unreasonable, people being obnoxious in a theater, someone who you think is unsuitable winning an election, or when you are standing in a line that won't move. During this week do the exercise at least three times a day. At bedtime, mentally review these situations. If you have not done it three times, recall at least three instances during the day in which you could have applied the technique and mentally rehearse it.

How it works

Throughout the day, whenever you get frustrated with or worried about a situation use this technique.

Whenever you are frustrated or worried, ask yourself these two questions:

- Is the outcome under my total control?

(If YES, you have nothing to worry about. Do whatever you need to do.)

- If not, is there any action that might influence the outcome under my control?

(If YES, take action on the aspect that is under your control.)

A few examples:

An interview

You have an important interview coming up and you are worried that you may not do well.

Is the outcome (getting the job) under your total control?

No. It is not. There may be a candidate who is better qualified, the interviewer may be biased against you, or they may already have decided on a candidate. Since it is not under your total control, it is nothing to you.

Is any action under your control?

Preparing for the interview well is under your control, whether it is well-received or not. So, act to prepare for the interview the best you can and do not worry about the results.

Missing your flight

You are driving to the airport. You started on time to get to the airport. But there is a huge traffic jam. It is almost certain that you will miss your flight.

Is the outcome (getting to the airport on time) under your total control?

No. It depends whether the traffic starts moving in the next few minutes. That's not under your control. So, it is nothing to you.

Is any action under your control?

Just relaxing is under your control. Listening to music or some inspirational talk is under my control. Planning for the next thing you have to do is under your control. You can relax and choose one of these activities.

Being diagnosed with an illness

You are diagnosed with diabetes.

Is the outcome (not having diabetes) under your total control?

No. You already have it. So, it is nothing to you and there is no point worrying about it.

Is any action under your control?

Collecting more information on the best course of action is under your control. Making the lifestyle recommendations suggested by your doctor is under your control. Seeing a movie you have been waiting to see is under your control. You can do these things rather than feeling sorry for yourself.

Daily quotes. week 4

The most important idea in this lesson is that we should act when things are under our control. Even when the outcome is not under our control, there may be aspects that may be under our control. We should identify anything that may be under our control and act on it. While this is implied in the dichotomy of control, it is not spelled out. So, there are not many direct quotes on the subject. What follows is a set of quotes related to the importance of action, not necessarily related to the lesson directly.

Sunday

Use what is given to you.

Epictetus, *Discourses* 2.16.28 (Chuck Chakrapani, *Stoic Choices* Ch. 2)

Monday

In effectiveness, practice is superior to theory.

Musonius Rufus, *Lecture 5* (Chuck Chakrapani, *Stoic Lessons* Ch. 5)

Tuesday

When action is needed, focus on what is being done.

Marcus Aurelius, *Meditations*, 7.4 (Chuck Chakrapani, *Stoic Meditions*, Ch. 7)

Wednesday

Everything is strengthened and preserved by actions that reflect its nature

Epictetus *Discourses* 2.9 (Chuck Chakrapani, *Stoic Choices* Ch. 9)

Thursday

Nothing is difficult, so far out of reach, that the human mind cannot conquer it.

Seneca, *On Anger* 2.12.3

Friday

You must practice what is appropriate to each lesson.

Musonius Rufus, *Lecture 6* (Chuck Chakrapani, *Stoic Lessons* Ch. 6)

Saturday

Practice creates the habit that is the result of practicing the theory.

Musonius Rufus, *Lecture 5* (Chuck Chakrapani, *Stoic Lessons* Ch. 5)

PART II

THE WALLS
AND THE WIDOWS

We now have the foundations of our Stoic house. Now we need to build the walls and the windows. The four walls of the house represent the four special skills (also called four excellences or four virtues) and the three windows represent the three disciplines we need to practice Stoicism.

Stoics believed that we cannot achieve happiness just by going after whatever makes us happy at any time. This may lead to long term unhappiness. Suppose food and drink make us happy. If you we keep eating and drinking without restraint, we may become obese and alcoholic, not conducive to a happy life. So, the Stoics said, we should acquire four special skills (excellences or virtues)—practical wisdom, justice, moderation, and courage—to be really happy. These are the four outer walls of the Stoic house. You can also think of them as four filters you have to put your judgments through to make sure that they pass the test. And, we need to practice three disciplines; assent, action, and desire. These are the three windows.

Filter 1. Practical Wisdom: What to Do and What Not to Do

Lesson 5

Big idea 5. Examine impressions before accepting

Instead of doing this one thing right—managing impressions to arrive at the right conclusion—we burden ourselves with many things ... We concern ourselves with so many things that they weigh us down.

Epictetus, *Discourses* 1.1.14-15 (Chuck Chakrapani, *Stoic Foundations*, Ch. 1)

The first wall of the house of Stoics is wisdom that comes from right judgments. Right judgments mean judging impressions the right way. The purpose of the first special skill of practical wisdom is to let us know *what to do* and *what not to do* in any given situation. (In some situations, it may not make any difference whether we act one way or another.)

Impressions are what we think about how things are, what is happening, what has happened or what will happen. You greet someone and the person doesn't acknowledge you. Your impression is that he is rude. The clerk at a corner shop shortchanges you. Your impression is she is dishonest and is trying to cheat you. Two or three things happen that are against your expectations. Your impression is that you are an unfortunate person.

Such impressions may or may not be correct. Yet we act on them as if they were true. When our impressions are incorrect, they lead to unhappiness. To be happy, we need to judge our impressions correctly.

Our impressions and reality

At the very beginning of this course we saw how our judgments and opinions affect our happiness. What do we base our judgments on? On what basis do we form our opinions?

We form our judgments and opinions based on what the Stoics called "impressions." In broad terms, all stimuli (and our unthinking interpretations of them) are impressions.

- You leave a restaurant late at night and start walking towards your home. The streets are deserted. You notice someone following you. You walk fast and so does he and, in a few minutes, he is very close to you. Based on your impression, your judgment is that he is a mugger. You decide to use pepper spray, kick him, and run away.

- Your boss—who is always cheerful and greets you when he sees you—is ignoring you today. You try to greet him; he sees it but does not respond. This impression leads to the judgment that your boss is not happy with you or is upset with you. You are unhappy for the rest of the day.

Impressions can lead to wrong judgments

Because we react based on our judgment of an event rather than an event itself, if our judgments are incorrect, our actions would be incorrect as well. Wrong judgments lead to wrong actions. In the two examples above, it is quite possible that the person following was not trying to hurt you and rob you. In the second example, your boss may be not unhappy with you.

But your judgments can also be wrong. In the first example, the person following you may be the waiter in the restaurant who is trying to catch up to you so he may return the wallet you left at the restaurant. The person following you deserves your thanks and not your attack. In the second example, your boss might have just received news that his wife was in an accident. Your judgment leads you to self-pity at a time you should be sympathetic to the other person.

When impressions are hard to judge

Some impressions are not difficult to judge. For example, yesterday you got into an accident and had whiplash. Clearly you cannot go back and avoid that accident (you can take no action) or not have whiplash (change the outcome). So, it is pointless keep worrying about. It doesn't make anything better. You can take no action and the outcome is not under your control. It is nothing to you.

Situation: You got into an accident yesterday	
Do you have control over ...	
Actions	No (The accident has already happened)
Outcome	No (You already have whiplash)

Sometimes, both action and outcome are under your control.

For example, you are angry at someone and you are about to say something hurtful to her, but you know that if you say it, it will only make things worse and won't make the situation any better. Do you have control over the action? Yes. As a result, you don't say it and so the outcome is also under your control.

What about something hurtful that happened yesterday? It is not under your control. But what you think about it today is under your control. It is easy to judge such impressions. But other impressions are hard to judge because we are led to believe that many things that are not true are true.

Suppose you train for a competition. You are particularly good at it. In fact, you are far superior to any of the other competitors. Is winning then under your control?

You are concerned about your heart health. You eat properly, maintain a healthy lifestyle, and exercise regularly. Is not getting a heart attack or stroke under your control?

You go to a motivational seminar. You are a junior executive in your company and the speaker tells you that you can absolutely be the president of your company if you follow his plan. Is becoming the president of your company under your control?

If you treat your spouse right and love him dearly, is there no way he will ever leave? Is this under your control?

We behave as though these things are under our control. Or believe that they are "somewhat" under our control. This makes people think of three categories or a "trichotomy" of control. But this is a misunderstanding. The outcome is fully under your control or it is not.

When we *believe* that the outcome is under our control, we set ourselves up for disappointments because it is not really under our control.

You may object. You may say that these things are *partly* under your control. Even if you cannot be certain of the outcome, you can increase the chances of achieving your desired outcome. What do we do in cases like that?

If you look more closely, you will see that the dichotomy of control doesn't change. When you believe that you have partial control, you will see that you have *complete control* over *what you can do* to influence the outcome; but still, you have *no control* over *the outcome* itself.

When the ancient Stoics were talking about the dichotomy of control, they were talking about the *outcome* of our actions, *not the actions* themselves. Outcomes are always either under our control or not under our control. Actions, on the other hand, are sometimes fully under our control (for example, getting upset about possibly missing the train), partially under our control (I can walk faster so I don't miss the train), and at other times not under our control (the train that has already left the station). The trichotomy of control is based on the confusion between actions and the outcome.

Let us look at the above situations more closely.

When an outcome is not under our control, *actions leading up to the outcome* may be under our control to varying degrees.

Missing the train

I missed the train. It has already left the station.

Action—I can do nothing to bring the train back: *Outcome*: not up to me.

Action	**Outcome**

Taking an Exam

My exam is next week. I am not well prepared, although there is still some time left

Action—I can do something, but not much: *Outcome*: not up to me.

Action	**Outcome**

Sports

I am participating in a sports completion. I am good and have plenty of time to prepare. I will continue to train until the last day

Action—I can do a lot; Outcome: not up to me.

Action	**Outcome**

All these situations have one thing in common. Whether the actions are up to me or not, the outcome is not up to me. Even if I have done something millions of times before, and am still capable of doing it now, such as crossing the street, the outcome is still not up to me. I may trip and break my foot, I may have a heart attack in the middle of the street, or I may be run over by a car. So, I take care when I cross the street (action that may be under my control) but, despite this, I can still be run over by a car driven by a drunk driver running a red light. The outcome is not up to me.

So, you can see that no matter how much (or how little) action is under your control, the outcome is not under your control because it depends on externals. It is a simple dichotomy. But your actions are— and always will be—under your control. You can use your power to act to *influence* the outcome, but not be certain you will achieve it. So, the outcome is nothing to you. But there are actions that would increase the chances of reaching your outcome. This is under your control. And we act as we learned in the previous training session.

A Stoic looks at every situation and realizes that if the outcome depends on others or outside events, it is not guaranteed. Many situations (but not all) have a component of things that are under your control. Acting on what is under your control will not guarantee the desired outcome, but it will increase it probability of its happening.

Judging impressions wisely

For this reason, we need the special skill of wisdom to tell us how to judge impressions the right way. The Stoics considered the skill of wisdom as one of the four cardinal virtues. Judging impressions correctly so we think and act the right way is a major part of wisdom.

We tend not to challenge our judgments. We don't pause to think whether they are right or wrong.

We don't distinguish them from reality. We think they are the same.

If someone avoids us, we may consider him arrogant. It doesn't occur to us he may just be shy. If someone is not paying attention to us, we assume that she does not care for us. We don't consider the possibility she may just be going through a difficult period in her life. If a couple of things go wrong in the morning, we generalize it for the entire day: "Today is not my day. Nothing is going well today." For the remainder of the day we go looking for instances where things did not go well for us.

The importance of judging impressions correctly

When we misjudge an impression, we distort reality. Decisions that follow from mistaken impressions tend to be unwise. Misunderstanding can poison friendships, punish the innocent, reward the guilty, destroy opportunities, and breakup marriages. We cannot flourish if our life is not aligned with reality.

How to judge impressions correctly

To judge impressions correctly, we must be rational in our thinking. In the previous four lessons, we talked about rationality from a Stoic perspective. To be rational, we should be clear about the four principles of reality.

- Our mistaken judgments create our unhappiness.
- When our judgments clash with reality, our life doesn't flow smoothly.
- There is no point in trying to fix what is beyond our control.
- The road to happiness lies in acting on what is under our control.

So, whenever you feel unhappy, apply the four principles, before coming to a judgment and acting upon it.

Principle 1. Stop and think: It is your judgment about the event that is causing you unhappiness.

Principle 2. Therefore, it stops you from having a smoothly flowing life.

Principle 3. Ask yourself if the event is under your control. If it is not, it is nothing to you. Move on.

Principle 4. If it (or any part of it) is under your control, decide to act on that.

A large part of wisdom is to think and act rationally. Therefore, wisdom is the consolidation of what we learned and practiced in the earlier four lessons.

The importance of wisdom

The special skill of wisdom is the first of four cardinal virtues. It can also be considered the most critical because it brings rationality with it and feeds into the other three special skills: justice, moderation, and courage. Wisdom and rationality are at the core of Stoic ethics. We need both rationality and wisdom to achieve happiness.

Key takeaways

1. *Our mistaken judgments create our unhappiness, because they clash with reality.*
2. *Practical wisdom shows us how to judge our impressions correctly.*
3. *There is no point in trying to fix what is beyond our control. The road to happiness lies in* acting on what is under our control.

Selected Readings

1. Use reason to evaluate impressions

[FROM Epictetus *Discourses* Bk 1.20; Chuck Chakrapani. *Stoic Foundations*, Ch. 20]

Nature has given us reason to test impressions.

"Why has nature given us the faculty of reason?"

"To make proper use of impressions."

"What is reason itself?"

"It is a collection of various impressions. Nature made reason capable of examining itself."

"To examine what? Why are we given this wisdom?"

"To examine what is good, what is bad, and what is neither. So, what is wisdom?"

"A good thing."

"And foolishness?"

"A bad thing."

"You see then that wisdom can examine itself and its opposite."

Do not accept untested impressions

For that reason, our most important job is to test our impressions and accept only those that pass the test. We believe our interests are affected by money. So, we have developed the art of assaying if coins are counterfeit: by sight, touch, smell, and hearing. The assayer drops a silver coin and listens closely to its ring. Not once but many times. By frequent attention to it, he has become quite a musician. Similarly, whenever we believe it makes a difference whether we get something right or wrong, we must play close attention and distinguish those things that might mislead us.

But when it comes to our poor ruling faculty, we yawn and go back to sleep, accepting every impression that comes our way. It does not occur to us that this will affect us in any way.

Do you want to know how unconcerned you are about what is good and bad and how eager you are about things that are indifferent? Compare your attitude towards physical blindness with blind judgments. You will see that you are far from having the feelings that you should have in relation to good and evil.

"But this requires long preparation, much effort, and study."

"So what? Do you expect to master the greatest of arts with little study?"

---

2. Understand different types of impressions and act accordingly

[FROM Epictetus *Discourses* Bk 1.27; Chuck Chakrapani. *Stoic Foundations*, Ch.27]

Impressions come to us in four ways

There are four types of external impressions

- Things are and they appear to be.
- Things are not and do not appear to be.
- Thing are, but do not appear to be.
- Things are not, but appear to be.

An educated person should judge impressions correctly in all these cases.

Find the right remedy for the right problem

If we find it difficult to judge impressions, we need to use the right kind of resources to find a solution.

If the sceptics (who, like Academics and Pyrrhonists, argue that we can know nothing for certain) bother us with their sophisms, let us seek remedy for that.

If we are concerned about the plausibility of things—when things appear good when they are not—let us seek a corrective for that.

If we are troubled by our habits, let's find a remedy for that. What aid can we find against habit? The contrary habit. Ignorant people commonly say, "He died. Poor man. His father died, his mother too. He died before his time, somewhere abroad." Listen to all that but distance yourself from such statements.

Check each habit with a contrary habit. If sophistry, then the art of reasoning. Against false impressions, we should have clear preconception, polished and ready for use.

---

3. Be understanding of others' misperceptions

[FROM Epictetus *Discourses*, 1.28; C. Chakrapani. *Stoic Foundations*, Ch. 28]

When people act on mistaken beliefs, we should not be angry with them

So, if someone agrees to what is false, we can be sure that she doesn't do so willingly (as Plato says, our mind is deprived of truth against its will), but it appears so to that person.

"In terms of action, do we have anything corresponding to true or false perceptions: What is our duty and what is not, what is beneficial and what is not, what is appropriate and what is not and so on?"

"A person cannot think of something as being of benefit to her and yet not choose it. Agreed?"

"But what about Medea who said, 'I know what I intend to do is evil; but my sober thoughts are overpowered by my passion'?"

"In her case, it is no different. She believed that gratifying her anger by taking revenge on her husband was more beneficial than saving her children."

"But she's wrong."

"Show her clearly where she went wrong, and she won't do it. But as long as you don't show it, what else has she got to go by, except what seems right to her?"

"Nothing."

"Why are you angry with her then? Poor woman, she is so confused about what is most important that, instead of being a human being, she has become a snake. Pity her instead."

We take pity on the blind and lame. Why don't we pity those who are blind and lame in their ruling faculty? Remember that our actions are the result of our impressions, which can be right or wrong. If right, you are innocent and if you are wrong, you pay the penalty. It is not as though if you go astray, someone else will pay the penalty. If you keep this in mind, you will not be angry or upset with anyone, won't insult, criticize, hate, or be offended by anyone.

"So, in your view, are great and dreadful deeds the result of sense impressions?"

"Yes. The result of that and only that."

Tragedies are the result of mistaken impressions

The *Iliad* is nothing but a sense impression and the poet's interpretation of it. An impression made Paris abduct Menelaus' wife and an impression made Helen follow him. If an impression had caused Menelaus to think that he was better off without her, then not only the *Iliad* would have been lost, but the *Odyssey* as well.

"Are you then saying that such great events depend on such a small cause?"

"Which of these events do you call great: Wars and factions, deaths of many men, destruction of cities? What is great about that? Nothing. What about slaughtering many oxen, sheep, burning a lot of storks' and swallows' nests?"

"Can you really compare the two?"

"They are very similar. In one case death happened to human beings and, in the other, to farm animals. People's houses were burnt in one case, storks' nests in the other. What is great or dreadful in all this? How is a house, merely a shelter, better than a stork's nest?"

"Are men and storks similar then?"

"There is a great similarity where the body is concerned. Only that in man's case his body lives in brick and mortar houses, while storks live in nests made of sticks and mud."

"So, there is no difference between a person and a stork?"

"Far from it. But not in these external things."

"In what ways do they differ, then?"

"Think about it. You will realize that humans differ in other respects: in their understanding of their actions, being sociable, trustworthy, honest, and intelligent and in learning from their mistakes."

"Where does good and evil come from then?"

"From things in which humans differ from animals. If you keep these qualities well protected, do not lose your honor, trustworthiness, or intelligence, then you are saved. But if you lose any of these qualities or if they are overtaken by turbulence, then you are lost."

All great things depend on this. Paris' tragedy was not that Greeks invaded Troy and killed his brothers. No, because no one falls because of the actions of others. What went on then was mere destruction of storks' nests. He fell when he lost his modesty, trustworthiness, respect for the laws of hospitality, and decency.

Similarly, Achilles' tragedy was not in the death of Patroclus. Not at all. It was when he gave in to anger, weeping over an insignificant woman, forgetting he was not there for romance but to wage a war. These are the ways in which human beings are defeated. This is the siege, the destruction of one's city, when a person's right judgments are torn down and destroyed.

Exercise 5. Epic Exam

When to use it

This is one of the most important Stoic exercises. Epictetus considered examining impressions as central to Stoicism. *For the rest of your life, no matter what other exercise you do, make sure you also do this exercise as well.* This exercise should become a part of your daily life. You should use it whenever you have an opportunity to do so.

Epic Exam is *not* an entirely new exercise, but a consolidation of the exercises we have done so far. The first four exercises dealt with the different components of rationality which, taken together, form the foundation for practical wisdom. Epic Exam combines all four aspects of rationality so we can examine impressions wisely and come to the right conclusions.

It is also particularly important for another reason. Although we study practical wisdom as a separate virtue, wisdom underlies the remaining three special skills (virtues).

How it works

Consider any situation with which you are unhappy. It could be "My spouse doesn't care for me anymore," "My boss thinks I am incompetent," "It's terrible, I lost my wallet," "I can't afford to go on a holiday this year," or "The restaurant may close before I get there."

Step 1: Pause for a moment. Understand that it is your thoughts creating your problem. You may be using the wrong handle.

Step 2: Think about what happened. State what happened with no commentary. (This is the impression without your judgment.)

Step 3. Ask if the event is under your control or not.

If it is not, it is nothing to you. Nothing to worry about. Do whatever is best to do.

If it is, then do what is needed. It is under your control, so there is nothing to worry about.

If the outcome is not under your control but there are some actions you can take to improve the chances of the desired outcome, take those actions.

Here are a few examples:

- Your performance review at work is tomorrow. You are worried about it. Is the review under your control and can you do anything to influence it now? No. Is there any action you can do about it? No. It is not under your control. It's nothing to you.
- Your performance review is 3 months away. You are worried about it. Is the outcome of the review under your control? No. It's not under your control. It is nothing to you.
- Is there any *action* you can take to improve your chances? Yes, you can do better work. Do that and don't worry about the outcome.
- You are angry at someone. It is bothering you. Is this under your control? Yes—you don't depend on anyone's permission to stop being angry. Do it.

The discipline of assent: The first window

In Stoicism, there are three disciplines: the discipline of assent, the discipline of action, and the discipline of desire. We practice the discipline of assent when we consider something and conclude whether it is true, false, or undecided.

In Epic Exam (this week's exercise), you examine whether something is under your control or not and, on that basis, you take your next action. This is an important part of practical wisdom. In applying Stoic wisdom, you give your assent to what is true, withhold your assent to what is not true, and suspend your judgment when you don't know if something is true or not.

This is an interesting point in Stoicism. As we saw at the very beginning of this course, Stoicism stresses the rational aspect of the human being. We can give assent to action that is in line with reality.

Stoicism does not deny our emotional nature. It simply says that we don't have to act as though we are helplessly held hostage by our emotions or irrationality. We feel the emotion like everyone else. But, as we experience our emotions, we realize that we have a choice to make. We can be carried away by our emotions and give assent to something irrational or we can choose to give assent to only what it true—things that will help us to flourish. Even if we do something that is contrary to reason at an emotional moment, we can still re-evaluate it and withdraw our assent to what is untrue.

Daily quotes. Week 5

Sunday

The most important task of a philosopher, his first task, is to test out impressions.

Epictetus *Discourses* 1.20.7 (Chuck Chakrapani, *Stoic Foundations* Ch. 20)

Monday

[You should] test out impressions and distinguish between them.

Epictetus, *Discourses* 1.20.7 (Chuck Chakrapani, *Stoic Foundations* Ch. 20)

Tuesday

[You should] not accept any impression unless it has been duly tested.

Epictetus *Discourses* 1.20.7 (Chuck Chakrapani, *Stoic Foundations* Ch. 20)

Wednesday

What does it mean to be getting an education?

It means distinguishing what is in our power and what is not.

Epictetus, *Discourses* 1.22.9 (Chuck Chakrapani, *Stoic Foundations* Ch. 22)

Thursday

By what aid, then, is possible against habit? The contrary habit.

Epictetus, *Discourses* 1.27.9. (Chuck Chakrapani, *Stoic Foundations* Ch. 27)

Friday

What is the reason we assent to anything? Because it appears to us to be so.

Epictetus, *Discourses* 1.28.1 (Chuck Chakrapani, *Stoic Foundations* Ch. 28)

Saturday

Remind me what you thought was good?

The will and the right use of impressions.

Epictetus, *Discourses* 1.30.4. (Chuck Chakrapani, *Stoic Foundations* Ch. 30)

Filter 2. Justice: Giving everyone their due

Lesson 6

Big idea 6. Be just

When we deal with others, we need a second skill—justice. What is justice? It is giving what is due to others, being fair in your dealings with them, and not taking anything that belongs to them. This is the second "wall" of our Stoic house.

Stoicism is very clear in saying that a person's happiness or unhappiness does not come from others. If it is true that no one can hurt us no matter what they do, it also follows that we can hurt no one, no matter what we do. So why be just? Why not steal, lie, cheat, or even commit murder for personal benefit?

Because it will hurt us.

Because we are first related to our family, then to our friends, then to the society we live in, and to the world, we are also a part of the universe. We cannot be unjust to others without it indirectly affecting ourselves. Since we are a part of society, when we hurt society, we hurt ourselves.

The rational principle that rules us has this quality: it is content with itself when it does what is just and thus achieves peace.

Marcus Aurelius, *Meditations*, 7.28 (Chuck Chakrapani, *Stoic Meditations*, 7.28)

Our relationship to others

The first skill—wisdom—taught us how to deal with ourselves; how to judge our impressions the right way and to decide on the next course of action. We need the skill of wisdom not only when we deal with ourselves but also when we deal with externals. Although wisdom of primary importance, we need additional skills as well.

The next skill we need relates to our interaction with others—those we know, those we don't, and, more broadly, the world at large. For Stoics, happiness does not depend on the place they live in. They are fully involved in this world. They don't retreat from it or go to a secluded place to find happiness. Their refuge is the "inner citadel" and not an outward place. Wherever they are—in their own city, in exile somewhere or in a prison—they are fully engaged in the world.

One of the basic beliefs of Stoicism is that we have a natural affection for others. It is natural, normal, and therefore necessary to cultivate concern for others and the world we live in.

Whatever is rational will not be in conflict with natural affection.

The two things cannot be in conflict.

Epictetus, *Discourses* 1.11 (Chuck Chakrapani, *Stoic Foundations* Ch. 11)

Our relationship to the world

When we take what is due to others, we are not acting in accordance with nature. We start believing external things such as injustice to others can bring us happiness. We create disharmony by putting our personal part in conflict with our universal part. Disharmony with nature cannot result in happiness. When we are in conflict with others, we are in conflict with ourselves. When we think we need something external (the main reason for injustice) or others don't deserve justice and act on that thought, we unwisely believe that externals will bring us happiness. Our life stops flowing smoothly. Hence the need for acting justly in our dealings with others.

The Stoic philosopher Hierocles thought of a person as being in the center of a set of concentric circles (the Hierocles circle, see the figure). Our relationship starts with ourselves and expands to include family, friends, neighbors, society, the city, the world, and the universe.

We are a part of the whole and therefore we are related to others and to the world. What is not good for others cannot be good for us.

What is not good for the beehive is not good for the bee.

M. Aurelius *Meditations*, 6.54 (Chuck Chakrapani, *Stoic Meditations*, 6.54)

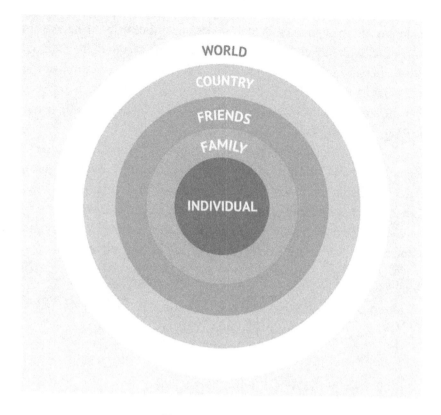

Figure 4 Hierocles Circles

Special skill: Justice

Since we are fully engaged in this world and are part of it, we don't turn away from others and what happens to them. The skill needed to realize this goal is called *justice*: to give others what is their due; to act in a way that doesn't assume we are more entitled to anything than anyone else; not to do or to desire things that are not ours; and not to believe that we need to harm anyone—because no one has anything we want or need—and to act in a way that is fair to everyone.

When we act unjustly, we believe that we stand to gain something by acting unjustly. But we have already seen that we can gain nothing from others, least of all by withholding what is due to them. Anything good, we need to get from ourselves. It is a part of our rationality (therefore according to nature) to appreciate our relationships to others and to act accordingly.

When we act unjustly and take what doesn't belong to us or do not give others what is due to them, we act as though we lack something that can be obtained by taking what doesn't belong to us or what is due to others.

> Let not your mind run on what you lack as much as on what you have already.
>
> Marcus Aurelius, *Meditations*

The role of justice in a life that flows well

The foundation of justice (especially as Cicero explained it) is that we wrong no one and promote public good. This means we should not harm anyone and should give everyone their due, even the most powerless in society, without expecting any reward in return.

How does this help us? Since there is nothing to be gained from being unjust and externals are nothing to us, there is no reason to be unjust. By being unjust, we can only damage the social fabric of which we are a part; we can only reinforce the belief that, by taking what doesn't belong to us, by not being fair to others, we can gain something for ourselves. We have already seen how unwise it is to believe that our happiness can come from others.

Our interdependence on other people and other countries, especially in these modern times, is undeniable. Even if we ignore natural affection, there is still a case for understanding that we are indeed interdependent. Why we should consider ourselves as a part of the social fabric is illustrated by this story.

You walk into a room and see a group of people sitting around the table looking hungry and miserable. They are all starving, although there is plenty of food on the table. The problem is they are unable to feed themselves because they all have spoons that can reach the food but are too long to reach their mouths. You walk into another room that looks exactly the same. But the people here are well fed, and they are happy and are conversing with each other. The difference? In this room, people are feeding each other, even though they can't feed themselves. We will probably never be in a situation like this, but in modern life our interdependence is undeniable.

When we act unjustly, we fail to see the resources we have within ourselves that could solve all our problems. Instead, we assume that, by being unjust, we could solve our problems or gain something that will increase our happiness, which can never be. Even if by being unjust we gain something temporarily, the advantages may not last long. Our unjust behavior may work against our long-term interests. Using our first skill of practical wisdom we see that such behavior will take us away from our goal of "a life that runs smoothly." And we see that justice is an important tool in making our life flow well.

I find delight in keeping my reasoning mind clear. By not turning away from human beings and what happens to them. By seeing and accepting everything with kindness, dealing with them as they deserve.

Marcus Aurelius, *Meditations*, 8.43 (Chuck Chakrapani, *Stoic Meditations*, 8.43)

Justice in everyday living

When we think of justice, we apply it to things that are obviously just or unjust. However, we are often unjust in small ways without every realizing it. We may not think that thoughts like, "this person does not deserve a promotion," "she could have tried harder," "if only he had done this..." are in fact unjust because we do not give a person what is their due. When we gossip about others without knowing all the facts, we are indulging in a form of injustice that could harm a person. In asking yourself the question "Is this unjust?" make sure that you understand we are often unjust in many subtle ways.

You are still afraid that others can harm you. You are not yet giving. You are not yet convinced that justice is the only wisdom.

Marcus Aurelius, *Meditations*, 4.37 (Chuck Chakrapani, *Stoic Meditations*, 4.37)

Kindness and compassion as a part of justice

In broad terms, justice includes kindness and compassion. It is the realization that all beings want to be happy and do things that they *think* will make them happy. Although we may often get the feeling that others are deliberately doing things to harm us they are mostly doing what they think is the right thing to do in running their lives. There is no need to impose our views on anyone. There is no need to be angry or upset with anyone. We deal with everyone and accept everything with kindness and compassion.

Everything I do—either by myself or with someone else—should have only one purpose, doing what is useful and well suited to all.

M. Aurelius, *Meditations*, 7.5 (Chuck Chakrapani, *Stoic Meditations*, 7.5)

Social action and justice

What about social action when we see something to be socially unjust? Should we speak up? Should we protest? From a Stoic perspective, if it is not our doing, it is neither good nor evil. If it is outside of us, we don't need it for happiness.

At first blush, then, it would seem that Stoics need not care for others. However, from the Stoic perspective we are part of the system which, starting from us, extends to the entire universe. So, when we act, we act not only for our benefit, but the benefit of our relatives, friends, and society at large.

As we act, we also keep in mind that the outcome is not under our control. Our wisdom tells us that, even when the outcomes are not under our control, our actions often are. When we can, we act. When we act, we put our proposed action through four filters the second of which is justice. We don't act as though the end justifies the means. Rather, we act with the means we have, acknowledging full well that we may not achieve our end at all. If it doesn't work out the way we would like, it is nothing to us. Not because we don't care, but because we have done all we can in good faith, but we don't control the outcome.

> To be drawn towards injustice, indulgence, anger, grief, and fear is a revolt against nature.
>
> Marcus Aurelius *Meditations*, 11.21 (Chuck Chakrapani, *Stoic Meditations*, Book 11.21)

Key takeaways

1. We have a "natural affection" for those close to us.
2. We are a part of the world and so our relationship extends from those who are close to us to the entire world.
3. Because of our interconnectedness we can't harm others without harming ourselves.
4. Not harming others means that we act justly towards others and the world in general. Justice is a cardinal Stoic virtue (special skill).
5. Justice includes not taking what doesn't belong to us, giving what is due to others, and being kind and compassionate to everyone.

Selected Readings. Week 6

While we have access to the writings of the Roman Stoics such as Musonius Rufus, Seneca, Marcus Aurelius, and Epictetus, the writings of earlier Stoics are lost. The Roman Stoics talk about justice, but they don't explain it. In particular, Marcus Aurelius refers to it several times. But even he doesn't explain why it is important. Perhaps it was self-evident to them.

The most important work on justice by a Stoic was written by Panaetius the last Scholarch of Stoicism. His work is now lost, and the only other source is *On Duties* by Cicero, a non-Stoic.

While Cicero (who was born several decades after Panaetius died) based his work on Panaetius' *On Duties*, he did not follow him completely. So, we don't have a Stoic source for our reading this week.

Instead we present a series of short extracts from Marcus Aurelius' Meditations and from Cicero's *On Duties*.

1. Dedicate yourself to the service of justice

[FROM M. Aurelius, *Meditations* 10.11,C. Chakrapani, *Stoic Meditations*, 10.11)

Acquire the ability to see how one thing changes into another. Constantly observe it. Use it to train yourself. Nothing will elevate your mind more because you realize that, at any moment, you may have to leave everything behind you, including the company of your friends and relatives.

From then on, you dedicate yourself wholly to the service of justice in whatever you do and nature in everything else. What people think or say or do against you is no longer your concern. Only two questions concern you now: Is what you are doing the right thing to do? Do you gladly accept whatever is given to you? All your cares and distractions are gone. You only want to walk the straight path of (the divine) law.

All virtues depend on justice

[FROM M. Aurelius, Meditations 11.10, C. Chakrapani, Stoic Meditations, 11.10]
Nature is never inferior to art since art is no more than an imitation of nature. Nature, which is most perfect and all-inclusive, cannot fall short of the artificial in its craftsmanship. All arts do the inferior things for the sake of the superior. So does the universal nature. Here then we find the origins of justice. All other virtues depend on it. We can never achieve true justice if we go after middle [indifferent] things, are or easily deceived or careless and changeable.

Justice is the only wisdom

[FROM M. Aurelius, *Meditations* 4.37, C. Chakrapani, *Stoic Meditations*, 4.37]
Very soon, you will be dead. Even so, you are not single-minded and peaceful. You are still afraid that others can harm you. You are not yet giving. You are not yet convinced that justice is the only wisdom.

Human beings are naturally just

[FROM M. Aurelius, *Meditations* 8.39, C. Chakrapani, *Stoic Meditations*, 8.39]
In the way human beings are made, I see no virtue placed in them to counter justice, but I see one to counter the love of pleasure: self-control.

About justice

[FROM Cicero, *On Duties*]

1. Justice consists in doing no injury to others.
2. Those who say that we should love our fellow citizens but not foreigners destroy the universal brotherhood of humanity, without which benevolence and justice would perish forever.
3. Justice is indispensable for the conduct of business.
4. Let the force of arms give place to law and justice.

Exercise 6. Fab Four

When to use it

Use this technique whenever you are tempted to be unjust to others for whatever reason: to gain an advantage over others, to get even with someone, because the other person is far too weak to retaliate, you are afraid, you cannot be bothered to be just, when you try to turn away from being kind or compassionate, or when you think it doesn't matter.

When we are tempted to be unfair for whatever reason, we often believe that it is to our advantage to do so. But it doesn't give us any lasting advantage. It is a lapse in rationality. How do we get back to being rational, wise, and just? To get back to rationality, Marcus Aurelius suggests that we ask ourselves to remind ourselves of four things. We call it the fab four.

How it works

Whenever you are tempted to act unjustly or fail to act to justly remind yourself of these four realities:

1. This thought of injustice is **unnecessary**.
2. This thought is **destructive** to my fellowship.
3. This is **not my true thought.** (It is out of place because it does not come from my heart and I really don't want to be unjust.)
4. (**Act justly** without blaming yourself.) When you are tempted to blame yourself, your divine part is beaten by your body, the inferior and perishable part.

Please remember, that these four realities apply to even simple forms of injustice such as being judgmental about other people's success and failures, being envious because others have something that we don't, or gossiping about others, which may have a negative impact. Do these exercises in all such circumstances.

Discipline of action: The second window

This brings us to the second discipline of Stoicism: the discipline of action. We don't act in ways that are unjust. We give others their due. We try to relieve the suffering of others when we can.

But we do none of these expecting things to change. We hope they will, but we know they may not. But we are not overly concerned about it. We act because it is the right thing to do. We act because we are part of this universe; if it is not good for the universe or for the society, it cannot be good for us.

Yet, we don't give in to righteous indignation. We are neither angry when we act nor upset if our actions don't change anything. We act because it is the rational thing to do. When we act rationally, our life runs smoothly.

We don't act justly expecting any reward. We act to change things, we act to alleviate suffering, and to bring about societal change. We act because we are interconnected with the world.

We act as a result of assenting to an impression.

This is the discipline of action.

Quotes for week 6

Sunday

Justice gives everyone their due.

Cicero, *On Duties*

Monday

The foundations of justice: no one should suffer wrong; then, that the public good be promoted.

Cicero, *On Duties*

Tuesday

The function of justice: not to do wrong to one's fellow human beings and not to wound their feelings.

Cicero, *On Duties*

Wednesday

Justice must be observed even to the lowest.

Cicero, *On Duties*

Thursday

Justice extorts no reward, no kind of price; she is sought...for her own sake.

Cicero, *On Duties*

Friday

This is our special duty, that if anyone specially needs our help, we should give him such help to the utmost of our power.

Cicero, *On Duties*

Saturday

Justice consists in doing no injury to men. Decency in giving them no offense.

Cicero, *On Duties*

Filter 3. Moderation: What to select and what not to select

Lesson 7

Big idea 7. Be moderate in your desires

There is no logical place where our desires end. Most of our desires are not extinguished when we fulfil them. Instead, they lead to greater and greater desires. So, the first problem with intense desires is that the more you feed them, the more you need them. The second problem with excessive desires is that when you are a slave to your desires, you become a slave to people who control what you desire.

This is not to say that you should lead an ascetic life and not enjoy the good things. But the best way to deal with desire is to neither resist nor avoid it. The special skill of moderation teaches us to tone down our desires, so they are fully under our control and we don't need anything outside of us to make us happy. We can then enjoy the good things in life without our becoming slaves to them or feeling deprived when we they are taken away from us.

This is the third special skill, moderation. This is knowing what to select, what not to select, and what does not matter.

> Why wait until there is nothing left for you to crave? That time will never come...There is a succession of desires; one is born from the end of another.
>
> Seneca, *Moral Letters* (Epistles) 118.6

Excessive desires make you a slave

Excessive desires make you a slave to the things you desire—be it alcohol, food, drugs, money, sex, power, or exotic experiences. For example, if you desperately desire public recognition, all your actions are influenced by this desire, no matter in what other ways it may damage you. If you desire security excessively, you become too afraid to explore any new possibility.

Excessive desires also make you a slave to people who have control over these things. You can become sycophantic or go along with unethical behavior if you think that it will get you what you want. Excessive desires are unhealthy because your desires start controlling you and you resemble a sick person.

> Don't you know how thirsty someone gets who is feverish? It has no resemblance to that of a healthy person. A healthy person drinks water and his thirst is gone. But a sick person feels all right for a while, feels nauseous, turns water into bile, vomits, bellyaches, and is even thirstier than before.
>
> Epictetus, *Discourses* 4.9.4-5 (Chuck Chakrapani, *Stoic Freedom*, Ch. 1)

Desires have no logical end

When we desire something, we are convinced that whatever we desire will bring us happiness. But once we get it, we find that it doesn't make us as happy as we thought it would. Yet we assume more of it would make us happy.

Would a million dollars make you happy? Would ten million? Maybe you already have a million or ten and probably you are no happier than you were when you were in school, or when you got your first job. You only need read about the rich—people who have earned more than they can spend in their lifetime—still craving for more, still constantly trying to acquire more, still trying to find happiness in drugs and alcohol.

That's the nature of desire. When you feed fire, it is not extinguished, but burns even more brightly and looks to consume more. As you eat more, you want to eat even more, becoming obese; as you drink more, you want to drink even more, becoming an alcoholic; as you earn more, you want to earn even more, sacrificing your social and personal life.

Not everyone who eats become obese, not everyone who drinks becomes an alcoholic, and not everyone who earns more becomes obsessed with money. But when you start desiring something very intensely, gradually it starts consuming your life. When a non-addict has a drink, he does so for the enjoyment of it; when an addict has a drink, he does so more to avoid the pain of not having a drink. Because desires have no logical end, we cannot hope to fulfill all our desires anyway.

Who was ever satisfied, after attainment, with that which loomed up large that they prayed for it?

Seneca, *Moral Letters* (Epistles) 19.

Natural desires and desires of opinions

There are two kinds of desires. Desires that are *natural* such as the desire for food when hungry or the desire for water when thirsty. And there are desires *born of our opinion*: we will be happy if we have so much money, such and such position, so many friends, so much sex, and so on. What is the difference between the two?

Natural desires are satisfied once you fulfil them. When you eat, you stop being hungry. When you drink water, you stop being thirsty. When you have a roof over your head, you feel protected. Natural desires have limits so you can fulfil them.

Desires born of your opinion are unlikely to be satisfied when you fulfil them. An expensive dress that you so desired and bought makes you happy. But only for a while. After a few months, not so much. You get the promotion you desired, you are happy for a while, but soon enough you will be looking for the next promotion. Those who desire a million dollars and get it will be looking for the next million, and those who desire a billion dollars and get it will be looking for the next billion.

Natural desires are limited; but those that spring from false opinion have no stopping point. The false have no limits.

Seneca, *Epistles*, 16,9.

Desires and envy

Because desires of opinion have constantly shifting goal posts, we compare what we have with what others have, to decide where the goal post should be. You may be happy with your income until you learn that your coworker—someone who you thought was half as good as you—is paid twice as much. You may be happy with your car until you see the fancy car bought by your neighbor.

Desires of opinions naturally generate envy. We acquire more and more, desire more and more when we see what others have. We value less and less what we have. What should make us happy doesn't *because* someone else has more of it.

No one who views the lot of others is content with their own.

Seneca, *On Anger* 3.31.1

The skill of moderation

So, to have joy and happiness that last, we should moderate our desires. We see how excessive desires trap us. Instead of being free, we become prisoners of our desires. So, the third skill or virtue we need to practice is moderation. This means we pursue our desires to the extent they don't start controlling us.

In practical terms, what does that mean? We can use the following guidelines to understand and moderate our desires, so we use our desires rather than be used by them.

- There are natural desires, such as quenching thirst or hunger. It is rational to fulfil such desires.
- There are desires compatible with wisdom and justice, such as the desire to earn a living to provide for oneself and others. It is also rational to fulfil such desires.
- Then there are desires that are neither natural nor related to wisdom or justice, such as the desire for gourmet food or drink, or good clothes, or a nice house. These desires, by themselves, are neither good nor bad. You can pursue such desires provided (a) you don't believe that they are needed for your happiness; (b) you are not driven by what others have; and (c) you are not bothered if you don't attain them or, after having attained them, they are taken away from you. This is the skill of moderation.

You indulge in pleasure, I use it. You think it is the highest good, I do not even think it to be good. For the sake of pleasure I do nothing, you do everything.

Seneca, *On the Happy Life*, 10 (Chuck Chakrapani, *Stoic Happiness*, Ch 10)

Key takeaways

1. *Our desires have no logical end. Satisfying one desire creates another. Fulfilling that desire creates another desire. The cycle keeps repeating because desires have no logical end.*

2. *Fulfilling all our desires is not in our best interest. Some of them (such as excessive eating or drinking) are likely to bring us pain in the end.*

3. *Even fulfilled desires won't bring us as much joy as we anticipate. Even if they do, we will get used to them fairly quickly.*

4. *Fulfilling desires to make others admire us will not work either. It might in fact create envy in others.*

5. *Our desires make us a slave of those who control what we want.*

6. *We generally have all we need but are constantly being held hostage by our desires.*

7. *We can live much more happily if we moderate our desires.*

Selected readings. Week 7

1. We always want more even when we don't need it

[FROM Seneca, *Moral Letters* 16]

This also is a saying of Epicurus: "If you live according to nature, you will never be poor; if you live according to opinion, you will never be rich." Nature's wants are slight; the demands of opinion are boundless.

There is no end to our desires

Suppose that the property of many millionaires is heaped up in your possession. Assume that fortune carries you far beyond the limits of a private income, decks you with gold, clothes you in purple, and brings you to such a degree of luxury and wealth that you can bury the earth under your marble floors; that you may not only possess, but tread upon, riches. Add statues, paintings, and whatever art has been devised for luxury; you will only learn from such things to crave still greater.

Desires do not have a stopping point

Natural desires are limited; but those which spring from false opinion can have no stopping-point. The false has no limits. When you are travelling on a road, there must be an end; but when astray, your wanderings are limitless.

Unlimited desire is contrary to nature

Recall your steps, therefore, from idle things. When you want to know whether your desire is based upon a natural or upon a misleading desire, consider whether it can stop at any definite point. If you find, after having travelled far, that there is a more distant goal always in view, you may be sure that this condition is contrary to nature.

2. Exercise Self-Control

[FROM Seneca, *On Happiness* 16; Chuck Chakrapani *Stoic Happiness* Ch 16]
We shall have pleasure for all that, but we shall be its masters and controllers. It may win some concessions from us but will not force us into anything.

On the contrary, those who permit pleasure to lead the van have neither one nor the other. They lose virtue altogether and yet do not gain pleasure. They are possessed by pleasure. They are either tortured by its absence or overwhelmed by its excess. They feel unhappy if they don't have it and yet more unhappy if overwhelmed by it—like those who are caught in the sandbanks of Syrtes, left on dry ground sometimes and tossed into the ocean at other times.

We are prisoners of pleasures because we lack self-control

This happens because we lack self-control and secretly love evil. It is dangerous for one who seeks after evil, instead of good, to get it. Great pleasures are like the wild animals we hunt with hardship and danger; even when we catch them, we are anxious because they can tear us to pieces. They turn out to be great evils and take us as their prisoners.

Tasteless people call a person happy if he enjoys more numerous and varied pleasures and is thus a slave of more masters. Let me extend this analogy. A person who tracks wild animals to their dens and follows the tracks of wandering animals with his hounds, neglects far more desirable things and fails to fulfill his duties. A person after pleasure postpones everything else, disregards the first essential—liberty. He sacrifices it to his belly. He does not buy pleasure for himself either but sells himself to pleasure.

3. Moderate your desires

[FROM *Discourses* 3.9, 21-22; Chuck Chakrapani *Stoic Training* Ch. 9]
To you, all you have seems small. To me, all I have seems important. Your desires cannot be fulfilled. Mine already are. When children put their hands into a narrow-necked jar to get nuts and figs out, the same

thing happens. Once they fill their hand, they cannot get it out. They cry. Drop a few and you will easily get it out. You too should drop your desires. Don't set your heart upon too many things and you'll get what you want.

Exercise 7. Pause and Ponder

When to use it

Whenever you need to understand the true nature of desire, use the Pause and Ponder technique. This will guide you to examine your desire rationally instead of unthinkingly fulfilling your desire—something that can work against your interest long-term.

How it works

When you feel a desire for anything such as food or some expensive new toy, the first thing to remember is not to be carried away. Fulfilling a desire may be good (such as the desire to eat when you are hungry or the desire to go out on a sunny day) or not-so-good (such as having a third desert with your meal or a seventh bottle of beer). Take time to examine what appears to be so appealing to you. What you are telling yourself is that fulfilling your desire will make you happy.

Whenever you have a desire (especially if you are not sure whether it is a basic need) ask these questions:

- Will it last long enough?
- Will it harm me later so my future will become less pleasurable?
- Will it harm others?
- Am I doing it for others' (external) approval?

After these four questions, if you decide that fulfilling your desire is not in your (and others') long-term interest, moderate your desire and steer it towards desires that are harmless to you and others.

As you practice this, you will see that conscious self-control based on reason (as opposed to some rule) is itself pleasurable.

Here is an example:

1. *Will it last long enough?* You see a beautiful pair of shoes or a dress that you can hardly afford. Maybe you can put it on your credit card. You imagine how good you will feel wearing it and how others will admire it—it's all so pleasurable. But will it give you as much pleasure three months from now? How about all the shoes and dresses that you thought would gave you great pleasure when you first bought them, but you don't wear anymore? Do you still want to buy this now?

2. *Will it harm me later so my future will become less pleasurable?* Example: (a) I can still enjoy my fourth dessert now. But my excessive consumption of sugar can make me obese and lead to the health problems that go with it. Do I still want to eat it? (b) The seventh beer is still enjoyable. But my excessive consumption of alcohol can make me an alcoholic. It can create health, social, and economic problems later. Do I still want to drink it?

3. *Will it harm others?* Example: What I am about to buy is made by children who are forced into modern slavery in a third-world country. Is my desire so important to fulfil that it doesn't matter who is harmed?

4. *Am I doing it for others' (external) approval?* Example: This big house, this shiny car will give me great pleasure particularly because it will be admired by my friends and neighbors. Can your worth be determined by others? Who are they whose approval you seek?

Daily quotes. Week 7

Sunday

You cannot achieve freedom by fulfilling your desires, but only by eliminating them.

Epictetus, *Discourses* 4.1 (Chuck Chakrapani, *Stoic Freedom*, Ch.1)

Monday

A desire for money and power makes you miserable and submissive to others. But so does its opposite, a desire for leisure, peace, travel, and learning.

Epictetus. *Discourses* 4.4 (Chuck Chakrapani, *Stoic Freedom*, Ch.1)

Tuesday

Life's ups and downs do not matter. Be moderate in your desires, rather than suppressing your sorrows.

Seneca, *On Happiness*, 25 (Chuck Chakrapani, *Stoic Happiness*, Ch. 25)

Wednesday

For god's sake, how much better the things I feared than the things I desired!

Seneca, *On Happiness*, 4 (Chuck Chakrapani, *Stoic Happiness*, Ch. 25)

Thursday

Unless someone shows them the difference between what is normal desire and what is wild and never-ending, the more they are satisfied, the more insatiable they become.

Seneca, *On Happiness*, 13 (Chuck Chakrapani, *Stoic Happiness*, Ch. 13)

Friday

Reason gives us the ability to act or not act and to desire something or move toward or away from it by properly judging our perceptions or impressions.

Epictetus, *Discourses* 1.1.70 (Chuck Chakrapani, *Stoic Foundations*, Ch. 1)

Saturday

Practice one time living like someone who is ill, so you can live like a healthy person in another. Take no food, just drink water. Abstain from every desire at one time so as to be able to exercise your desires in a reasonable way at a later time.

Epictetus *Discourses*, 3.13, 21 (Chuck Chakrapani, *Stoic Training*, Ch. 13)

Filter 4: Courage: What Is Terrible and What Is Not Terrible

Lesson 8

Big idea 8. Face fears and aversions with courage

Almost all of us can see why excessive desires can harm us. We stay away from excesses because we know that things like excessive drinking, eating for greed, or excessive money may not be good for us. However, we don't realize that our aversions (what we fear and hate) are the flip side of our desires. Desires can control our life because we *desperately want* something and will do anything to get it. Our fears and aversions can control our life as easily because we *desperately don't want* something to happen and will do anything to avoid it. When we pursue something we desire, we believe that what we desire would bring us happiness. When we try to avoid something, we believe that avoiding it would bring us happiness. But the mechanism is the same for both.

A good way of understanding our aversions is to think of them as our *excessive desire to avoid* something. Looked at this way, our aversions are no different from our desires.

We need a special skill to deal with our fears or aversions. This special skill is courage. Courage is knowing what is terrible and what we should be afraid of, what is not terrible that we should not be afraid of, and what doesn't rally mater.

> It makes little difference whether you want to be a senator or not want to be one; whether you want to hold office or not want to hold office; whether you say, "I'm in a bad way. I can't do anything because I am tied to books," or you say, "I'm in a bad way. I've no time to read."
>
> Epictetus *Discourses* 4.4 (Chuck Chakrapani, *Stoic Freedom*, Ch. 4)

What are aversions?

In Stoicism, the term aversion includes a wide variety of things, ranging from your mild dislike of broccoli to your fear of death. Aversions include all fears, small or large—fear of illness, fear of old age, fear of loneliness, fear of death—all these are your aversions. If you were not averse to being ill, being old, being lonely, and dying, you wouldn't fear them.

Aversions are our dislikes, our "hates," our fears of different shades, our prejudices and the like. They are the flipside of our desires. When we desire something, we move *towards* it. We spend a lot of time and resources to get it. When we are averse to something, we move *away* from it. We spend a lot of time and resources to avoid it. The only difference between the two is the direction. To be happy not only do we need to moderate our desires, but we should also have the courage to face our aversions.

Aversions can take many forms. We avoid things we are averse to. They can be big or small:

- You cross the street to avoid talking to someone.
- You are fearful of public speaking.
- You hate broccoli.
- You are afraid to do things that you want to *because* of what others might think.

- You accept whatever your boss says *because* you think your career is depends on it. (You are averse to losing your job.)
- You avoid a person *because* he threatens to physically harm you or even to kill you.
- You want to live in a gated community *because* you are afraid others may hurt you.
- You are afraid of being lonely.
- You are afraid of old age.
- You are afraid of illness.
- You are afraid of dying.

Like desires, aversions are not a major problem if they are not intense or if they aren't too many. But, as we will see, they can become a problem when they are many or when they are intense.

We are ruled by our desires and aversions. When we desire something, we aim to get it. If we don't get what we desire, we feel disappointed.

Epictetus *Enchiridion*, 2 (Chuck Chakrapani, *The Good Life Handbook*, 2)

Why are aversions a problem?

Why are aversions a problem? What is wrong with avoiding things that are unpleasant or dangerous?

Actually, there is nothing wrong with avoiding things that are harmful or preferring one thing over another. In many cases, it may be the intelligent thing to do. If you see a speeding car when you are crossing the street, it is intelligent to get out of its way. If you are in a burning house, it is safer to get out quickly. If you are walking home at night, you may be better off avoiding rough areas.

The problem arises when we don't have control over things that might happen. If we are averse to what is almost certain such as illness, old age, or death, we are bound to suffer. When our aversions to external things are too many or too intense, two things happen: our world shrinks and we lose our freedom. Neither is conducive to the good life.

"Well, what's wrong with being here in a cage?"

"What a silly question! I was born to fly as I please, to live in the open air and sing. You want to take away all that from me and then ask, 'What's wrong with being here in a cage?'"

Epictetus, *Discourses* 4.1 (Chuck Chakrapani, *Stoic Freedom*, Ch.1)

Aversions can run your life, while your world narrows

The first reason to be careful about our aversions is that they shrink our world. When we are averse to many things –broccoli, crowds, loud people, foreigners, poor economic conditions, and the list can be very long—our choices narrow, and we are less free to act. Even when our aversions are simple and harmless (such as your dislike for broccoli or long queues), when we have too many of them, we try to avoid them and, as a result, start living in a prison of our own making

What is wrong with living in such a self-made prison? Maybe nothing, but the Stoics conceived a life of freedom, fearlessness, and openness—a life that is the opposite of being in a self-made prison. The Stoic way of life does not include living with unnecessary self-made restrictions.

The second reason to be careful about our aversions is that they are fears of things big and small; they start running our life. For example, let's say we are excessively concerned about job security. We become fearful of losing our job and do whatever it takes to keep it—even when what we do is unethical or conflicts with other values we cherish. Our fears—fear of losing our job, fear of losing our loved ones, fear of old age, fear of unfamiliar things and people, and the like—take over our life. Just as we lose our freedom when we give in to excessive desires, so we lose our freedom when we give in to excessive aversions.

There is no limit to our sorrows if we indulge our fears to the greatest possible extent.

Seneca, *Moral Letters* 13

Being averse to things we don't control

Another big problem with aversions is that most of them are externals and we don't control them. Things we are averse to include bad weather, loud people, job loss, uncaring friends, conniving family members, illness, or death. So, we often react in one of two ways to our aversions:

- Pay a high price to avoid the situation altogether; or
- Feel fearful, frustrated, or disturbed about the situation that is not under our control.

As we saw earlier, running away from a situation does not really solve the problem. It just makes our world smaller. Besides, even if we run away from this one, we may face a comparable situation soon enough. Feeling frustrated about the situation that we don't control is meaningless.

We are effective when we are averse only to things we control. If we are averse to crowds, what is it that we control and what is it that we don't control? We don't control the crowds so there is no point in being averse to them. But we control how we feel about them. So, we çan choose not to be annoyed by crowds and even welcome them.

If I free myself from emotions that make the master frightened, what troubles can I have?

Epictetus, *Discourses* 1.29 (Chuck Chakrapani, *Stoic Foundations* Ch.29)

Courage, the skill needed to deal with aversions

As we said before, there is nothing wrong in preferring certain things and not preferring certain things. Stoics don't invite danger or needlessly put themselves in unpleasant situations. But Stoics do not avoid dangerous or unpleasant situations if they believe something more important is at stake. If they must face unpleasant or dangerous situations, they are fearless and courageous.

This is Stoic courage: Not shrinking from facing situations that others would consider unpleasant or dangerous, if something more important is at stake.

What is "more important" than keeping yourself safe and free from danger? For the Stoics, it is whatever is in line with rationality and excellence. If it is not a rational thing to do, if not facing the situation will violate the basic virtues or excellences—wisdom, justice, or moderation—then courage is the special skill you need to act.

Stoic courage is also the courage to face the fact that most of what we fear is external to us and therefore nothing to us.

Because Stoics know that externals cannot harm them, they are more concerned about doing what is rational than avoiding externals to keep themselves physically safe. Safety may be important (a "preferred indifferent"), but it means nothing to them when more important things are at stake. Stoic courage is based on considerations such as:

- If something is totally out of our control, what is the point in being afraid of it?
- If what someone else does is not under our control, why be fearful of anyone?

If externals cannot harm us, why should we have an irrational fear about them?

So, the fourth special skill that a Stoic cultivates is fearlessness by not being averse to things not under their control. Stoic *courage* is being fearless in the face of aversions: not to be afraid of poverty, not to be afraid of public opinion, not to be afraid of disease or even death. A Stoic is not foolhardy, and a Stoic is not courageous for the sake of being courageous. A Stoic is fearless because she realizes that there is nothing to be afraid of.

Let another say. "Perhaps the worst will not happen." You yourself must say, "Well, what if it does happen?"

Seneca, *Moral Letters* 13

Key takeaways

1. Aversions are our fears and dislikes.
2. When we are averse to external things, we are trapped by what happens around us. We lose our freedom.
3. Aversions start running our lives and our world shrinks.
4. The special skill of courage is facing our external aversions and realizing that the only way to be free is to stop being averse to anything we don't control—whether it is disease, poverty, or even death.

Selected Readings. Week 8

1. Reframe your thinking to avoid aversion

[FROM Epictetus, *Discourses* 1.29; Chuck Chakrapani, *Stoic Foundations* Ch. 29]

Reframe your thinking to be in accordance with nature

Avoiding others is not possible. Nor do we have the power to change others. Then how do we deal with them? By understanding that people will act as they please, but we will act in accordance with nature.

That's not what you do though. You gripe and protest. When you are alone you say you are lonely. When you are with people, you find fault with them, even if they are your parents, children, spouse, and neighbors. What you should do instead is this: When you are alone call it peace and freedom; when you are in company, instead of calling it a crowd and being annoyed, call it a festival. Learn to enjoy it.

Misery is the penalty for not being in accordance with nature

What is the penalty for not accepting things the way they are? To be just the way you are; miserable when alone and unhappy when with others. There is no need to throw you in prison, you are already in one. Whatever place you are in, if you are there against your will, you are in prison. But even if you are in prison, if it is by your will, then you are free. This is the reason Socrates was not imprisoned, because he was there willingly.

So, what if my leg is crippled? It's just an insignificant leg. Do you want to blame the universe for it? Why not joyfully surrender your entire body to the one who gave it to you? Do you want to be angry and discontented with God, who designed everything at the time of your birth? Don't you realize your insignificance in the larger scheme of things? That is about the body. But, as far as reason is concerned, you are on par with God. The greatness of reason is not measured by size but by the quality of its judgments. So, would you rather not be equal to God?

You can cope with any situation

Are you discontented because of the parents you have? How would it have been possible for you to exist before your parents' time and say, "Let such a man make love to such a woman, so I can be born in a certain way." No, it would not have been possible. It was necessary for your parents to have existed before you were born.

"How so?"

"It's just the way things are."

"If so, don't you have any remedy?"

Well, if you don't know the purpose of sight, you might close your eyes as a beautiful painting passes by you and feel miserable. Are you less miserable not knowing you have the resources to cope with anything that may happen to you? You are given the faculty to cope with things. But you turn away from it at the very time you need it.

---

2. Quit complaining about your aversions

[FROM Epictetus, *Discourses* 1.6; Chuck Chakrapani, *Stoic Foundations* Ch. 6]

Quit complaining and realize your strengths

You may say unpleasant and difficult things happen in life. Quite so. Suppose you get to a beautiful place. Then what? Won't you get hot? Won't you find it crowded? Won't you get soaked when it rains? Won't it be noisy? Won't you find other irritations? Knowing all this, you still go there because you think the beauty of the place is worth it. Have you not received the inner strength to cope with any difficulty that may arise? Have you not been given strength, courage, and patience? Why then should you worry about what happens, when you are armed with these virtues and have the power to endure? What could constrain, compel, or even annoy you? You don't see all this. Instead you moan, groan, shed tears, and complain.

"But my nose is running."

"What do you have your hands for, idiot, if not to wipe it?"

"But why should my nose run in the first place?"

"Why waste your time protesting? Isn't easier just to wipe it?"

What would have become of Hercules, if there had been no lion, hydra, stag, boar, or brutal criminals? What would he have done without such challenges? Clearly, he would have wrapped himself and slept.

"In that case maybe he should have created these challenges for himself—such as searching for a lion, a boar, and a hydra to bring them into his land."

"It would be madness to create problems for ourselves so we can solve them. But the challenges that came Hercules' way proved useful tests of Hercules' nature and strength."

Now you know all this, appreciate all the resources you have. When you are done, say, "Let any difficulty come my way. I have the resources and a constitution given to me by my creator to deal with whatever happens."

But no, there you sit, trembling with fear about what might happen in the future and upset about things that are happening now. You blame God. How does such weakness help? Yet God has given you the strength to tolerate trouble without being humiliated. He has also provided you a means to be free of constraint, hindrance, or compulsion, without having to fall apart. You have all these powers given to you which God himself cannot take away. Yet you don't use them. You don't even realize what powers you have and where they came from. You refuse to acknowledge your creator and his gifts. Some of you don't even acknowledge his existence.

My challenge to you

I am ready to show you that you have resources, strength of character, and resilience. I challenge you to show me what grounds you have to complain and be reproachful.

3. Deal with your fears

[FROM Seneca. *Moral Letters* 13]

Most of our aversions and fears are groundless

More things are likely to frighten us than to crush us. We suffer more often in imagination than in reality. Some things trouble us more than they should; some trouble us before they should; and some trouble us when they ought not to trouble us at all. We exaggerate, or imagine, or anticipate, feel sorrow.

How to deal with our fears and aversions

You may retort with the question: "How am I to know whether my sufferings are real or imaginary?" Here is the rule for such matters:

We are tormented either by things present, or by things to come, or by both.

- As to things present, the decision is easy. Suppose you enjoy freedom and health, and that you do not suffer from any external injury.
- As to what may happen to it in the future, we shall see later on. *Today there is nothing wrong.*

"But," you say, "something will happen."

First, consider whether your proofs of future trouble are sure. For it is more often the case that we are troubled by our fears.

Put your fears to test

We do not put to the test those things which cause our fear; we do not examine them; we go pale and retreat just like soldiers who are forced to abandon their camp because of a dust-cloud raised by stampeding cattle, or are thrown into a panic by the spreading of some unauthenticated rumor. And somehow or other it is the idle report that disturbs us most. For truth has its own definite boundaries, but that which arises from uncertainty is delivered over to guesswork and the irresponsible license of a frightened mind. That is why no fear is so ruinous and so uncontrollable as panic. For other fears are groundless, but this fear is witless.

What you are afraid of may never happen

Let us, then, look carefully into the matter. It is likely that some troubles will befall us; but it is not a present fact. How often has the unexpected happened? How often has the expected never come to pass? And even though it is ordained to be, what does it avail to run out to meet your suffering? You will suffer soon enough, when it arrives; so, look forward meanwhile to better things.

What shall you gain by doing this? Time. There will be many happenings meanwhile which will serve to postpone, or end, or pass on to another person, the trials which are near or even in your very presence. A fire has opened the way to flight. Men have been let down softly by a catastrophe. Sometimes the sword has been checked even at the victim's throat. Men have survived their own executioners. Even bad fortune is fickle. Perhaps it will come, perhaps not; in the meantime, it is not. So, look forward to better things.

You have the resources to cope with whatever happens

Life is not worth living, and there is no limit to our sorrows, if we indulge our fears to the greatest possible extent; In this matter, counter one weakness with another, and temper your fear with hope. There is nothing more certain among our fears than the certainty that things we dread sink into nothing, and that things we hope for mock us.

Don't be frightened by uncertainties

We let ourselves drift with every breeze; we are frightened of uncertainties as though they were certain. We observe no moderation. The slightest thing turns the scales and throws us into a panic. Let another say, "Perhaps the worst will not happen." You yourself must say, "Well, what if it does happen? Let us see who wins. Perhaps it happens for my best interests; it may be that such a death will shed credit upon my life."

The discipline of desire: The third window

This is the last of the three disciplines we need to practice Stoicism.

Desires

When we desire something, we shouldn't unthinkingly indulge in it. Instead, we should first examine it to see if the desire is internal (for example, being kind to someone) or external (wanting a relationship with someone.)

If it is internal, then we are free to indulge in it so long as it passes the four filters: wisdom, justice, moderation, and courage.

If it is external, then we know it is an indifferent. So, we ask the question "Is it a preferred indifferent or a dispreferred indifferent?" If it is a preferred indifferent, we put it through the same four filters. If it passes, we are free to act. If it fails, then we moderate our desire. If our actions don't succeed in getting what we want, it is nothing to us, because it is an external.

Aversions (fears)

When we are averse to something or afraid of something, we don't unthinkingly run away from it. Instead, we first examine to see if the aversion and fear is internal (for example, "I would rather avoid stealing, even though I need the money") or external ("I am afraid I may not get the job unless I fudge my resume").

If it is internal, then we are free to indulge in it so long as it passes the four filters: wisdom, justice, moderation, and courage.

If it is external, then we know it is an indifferent. So, we ask the question, "Is it a preferred indifferent or a dispreferred indifferent?" If it is a preferred indifferent, we put it through the four filters. If it passes, we are free to act. If it fails, then we apply courage to get out of our fear or aversion. In fact, it is nothing to us.

This is the discipline of desire.

Exercise 8. Resources Review

When to use it

Use the Resources Review technique whenever you need to understand and diffuse your fear or aversion. This will enable you to counter your aversions and fears.

How it works

Whenever we face something we don't like, or something we are afraid of, we act helpless. We act as though we cannot do anything about the situation. We tend to forget the immense internal resources available to us. So, when you are afraid of or averse to a situation, ask yourself this question:

What resource do I have to cope with this situation I am afraid or fearful of?

Here are a few examples:

This line is too long. I am getting upset.

What resource is available to me to counter this? Patience. In the scheme of things, waiting in line for a few more minutes is not going to change anything.

Someone is talking loudly on the phone in the library

What resource is available to me to counter this? Compassion. I have done things in the past which might have annoyed others.

I am worried I will lose my job.

What resource is available to me to counter this? My resilience: I have been in many unpleasant situations before and survived them. I can survive this too.

I am afraid of death.

What resource is available to me to counter this? My wisdom. I know that I can do nothing about what I don't control. I have no control over death. Therefore, it is nothing to me.

My medical report was not good news.

What resource is available to me to counter this? My ability to act. In the past, I have faced many situations that were not to my liking and overcame them by taking proper action. Here, I will do everything I can to minimize the impact of current conditions. If I can't do anything, it is nothing to me anyway.

Daily quotes for week 8

Sunday

When we are averse to something, we want to avoid it. If we end up getting what we don't want anyway, we feel unhappy.

Epictetus, *Enchiridion*, 2 (Chuck Chakrapani, *The Good Life Handbook*, 2)

Tuesday

Direct your aversions only to things under your control.

Epictetus, *Discourses* 1.4, (Chuck Chakrapani, *Stoic Foundations* Ch. 4)

Wednesday

We identify ourselves with our bodily organs such as our stomachs and guts. Our fears and desires are shaped accordingly. We become vulnerable to fear and desire. We flatter those we think can help us and fear those we think can hurt us.

Epictetus, *Discourses* 1, 9 (Chuck Chakrapani, *Stoic Foundations* Ch. 9)

Thursday

Appreciate all the resources you have. When you are done, say "Let any difficulty come my way. I have the resources and a constitution given to me by my creator to deal with whatever happens."

Epictetus, *Discourses* 1, 6 (Chuck Chakrapani, *Stoic Foundations* Ch. 6)

Friday

If you are pained by anything external, the pain is not due to the external thing. It is due to the way you look at it. You have the power to change this at any moment.

Marcus Aurelius, *Meditations* 8.47 (Chuck Chakrapani, *Stoic Meditation*, 8.47)

Saturday

We magnify our sorrow, or we imagine it, or we get ahead of it.

Seneca, *Moral Letters* 13.5

PART III

THE ROOF

We have thus far talked about the foundations of Stoicism, the four walls (the four special skills or virtues), and the three windows (the three disciplines.) This covers the fundamental aspects of Stoicism. But we need to carry this knowledge into our everyday living and enjoy the festival of life (the roof of our Stoic house). The two chapters in this section deal with applying Stoic principles to our daily lives.

Living Everyday

The lesson

Big idea 9. Practicing everyday is the best way to make the ideas readily available

When we are in the grip of negative emotions, worries, and anxieties, fear can still take hold of us and cloud our judgment, even if we practice Stoicism regularly. We can deal with these problems by knowing that we have resources available for whatever life may throw at us and remembering that we are more resilient than we think.

As we keep practicing these principles, we realize nothing can harm us except ourselves. We start to see things as they really are, a procession of kaleidoscopic events. Some of the kaleidoscopic events may look scary but, in the end, are powerless to harm us—until we give them that power.

When we start seeing life and others as incapable of harming us, a gentle sense of humor and compassion replaces our constant caution and the frequent sense of hurt. We become confident that we will always have the resources needed to cope with life. We set down the heavy burden of our imagined universe that we thought was always ready to hurt us.

What is death? A scary mask. Take it off. See, it doesn't bite… What is pain? A scary mask. Turn around and look. Our flesh is affected by impressions—sometimes hard and sometimes smooth.

Epictetus *Discourses* 2.1. (Chuck Chakrapani, *Stoic Training*, Ch. 1)

Being compassionate

One of the basic misconceptions of Stoicism is that it is cold, unfeeling, emotionless, and therefore uninvolved. This perception may be due to the fact that the ancient Stoics used the word "passion" to denote negative emotions. It is easy to mischaracterize the Stoics as "dispassionate" and therefore withdrawn. Not so. The ancient Stoics were cosmopolitans who were actively engaged with life and sought to help others.

Help those in need as far as you can. They deserve it.

Marcus Aurelius, *Meditations* 5.35 (Chuck Chakrapani, *Stoic Meditations*, Ch. 5.35)

They helped others not just because it was their duty to do so as a part of humanity but also because they were sympathetic to other people's difficulties, without necessarily identifying themselves with others' problems.

I should not be unfeeling like a statue but should take care of my natural and acquired relationships—as a human being who honors gods, as a son, as a brother, as a father, as a citizen.

Epictetus, *Discourses* 3.2.4 (Chuck Chakrapani, *Stoic Training*, Ch. 2)

Their compassion for others was not diminished even though they knew that everyone is responsible for their own happiness. When somebody is grieving,

Be careful not to show disdain for their grief. Show them sympathy, use comforting words, and even share their misery outwardly.

Epictetus, *Enchiridion* 16 (Chuck Chakrapani, *The Good Life Handbook*, 16)

And, as a result they valued fellow feeling, humanity, and sociability.

This is the first premise that philosophy holds out to us: fellow feeling, humanity, sociability.

Seneca, *Moral Letters*, 5-4.

As a Stoic, you are not withdrawn but are vigorously engaged in society, you will be subject to emotions like everyone else, no matter how long you practice. But the grip of negative emotions will not last long. Neither will it be vise-like.

Being less than perfect

So, if you practice Stoicism, will you never be angry, upset, or fearful?

Not really. You can practice Stoicism all your life and yet your first reaction to someone coming at you with a knife can be fear; you will still feel startled by some unexpected commotion; you will still feel sad when a loved one dies; and you will still feel panic when there is severe turbulence when you fly. All these are natural.

A courageous person will frown at sad things; will be startled by a sudden occurrence; will feel dizzy when looking down, if standing at the brink. This is not fear, but a natural feeling not to be overcome by reason.

Seneca, *Epistles*, 57.4

So, you don't have to be embarrassed if you feel anger or fear. Your initial reaction to an impression is not that of your rational mind.

Whatever is implanted and inborn can be reduced with practice, but not overcome.

Seneca, *Epistles*, 11.1

Being resilient

While most people get carried away by their fear or anger, the Stoics consider it as an "impression." Impressions can be deceiving. Once the initial reaction of panic, fear, or anger occurs, the Stoic says to herself: "Let me examine the true nature of this," and puts the impression through Epic Exam (Week 5.) She realizes that there is no need to panic, be angry or fearful. Rationality takes over and she looks for the best course of action rather than being dumbstruck by whatever happens. If our first reaction is to retaliate when we think someone has harmed us, soon enough we use reason and calm down, rather than reacting in foolish and unproductive ways.

> You think yourself injured and want to seek revenge. And then you are persuaded against it by reason. You calm down again quickly. I don't call this anger, but a mental impulse giving in to reason.
>
> Seneca, *On Anger*, 2.3.1-2,4

It is the same with other negative emotions such as fear. Our first reaction may be to be fearful of things but then we use reason and see things differently.

Living in the present

We often imagine what might happen in the future and become worried. We live in fear of myriad things: we may lose our job, may not have enough money, may become ill, our life won't amount to anything, and so on. But as Michel de Montaigne put it, "My life was filled with terrible misfortunes, most of which never happened."

> There are more things that frighten us than affect us. We suffer more often in our imagination than in reality...We magnify our sorrow, or we imagine it, or we get ahead of it.
>
> Seneca, *Epistles*, 13.4-5

But what if things do not turn out the way we want, and we face misfortunes? The first answer to this question is that we will still have the same resources we had thus far to run our lives. They will carry us forward in the future and there is no need to worry in advance of anything happening. As a rational person, you can plan for the future, but if things turn out to be different, as a Stoic, you can still cope with whatever happens.

> Don't let the future worry you. You will meet it—if you have to—with reason, the resource you now use to deal with life.
>
> Marcus Aurelius, *Meditations* 7.8 (Chuck Chakrapani, *Stoic Meditations*, 7.8)

Being light with a sense of humor

When we gradually begin to understand that nothing external can harm us, our worries, anxieties, and fear start losing their grip on us.

As we learn not to value anything external, we are not afraid of losing anything. Since we don't feel we can be harmed by anything external, we find we have nothing to lose, nothing to complain about. We find it unproductive to add anger and upset to life's predicaments. We free ourselves from carrying the emotional load all the time and we set it down. We become light.

> Nothing is heavy if we take it lightly. Nothing needs provoke anger if you do not add your anger to it.
>
> Seneca, *Epistles* 12.3.1

How humorous were the ancient Stoics? We really cannot say. They did not write jokes. They lived before the age of stand-up comics and sitcoms. Ancient Stoics lived in difficult conditions with threats of exile, confinement, and arbitrary death constantly hanging over them. As Seneca put it,

> Sometimes even living is an act of courage.
>
> Seneca

Yet we can get some glimpse of their cheerfulness, humor (often expressed as mockery), and a sense of irony by their writings and by anecdotes about them.

- Chrysippus is said to have died laughing at the age of 73.
- When Alexander the Great asked Diogenes whether he could do anything for Diogenes, he replied "Yes, get out of the way. You're hiding the sun."
- "If you have your heart set on wearing crowns, why not make one out of roses—you will look even more elegant in that." (Epictetus)
- It is the mark of a greater mind not to restrain laughter ... laughter expresses the gentlest of our feelings and reckons nothing is great or serious.
- We should make light of all things ... It is more civilized to make fun of life than bewail it. (Seneca)
- The mind should not be kept continuously at the same pitch of concentration but given amusing diversions. (Seneca)
- He who laughs at humanity deserves better of it than he who mourns for it. (Seneca, 15)

We will not find anything "laugh-out-loud funny" in ancient Stoic writings. (This is not just true of the Stoics—Socrates, Plato, Aristotle, and others weren't side-splittingly funny either.) What we will find is their sense of humor, expressed gently though irony, sarcasm, and self-deprecating humor.

> No one is laughed at who begins by laughing at himself.
>
> Seneca, *On the Firmness of a Wise Person*, 17

Dealing with negative emotions

Our practice over the past eight weeks should have given us the means of coping with anything that comes our way. However, even if your practice has been successful, there will be times when your initial reaction to a situation could be one of anger, despair, or fear. In fact, such a reaction can linger for a while. It's one thing to visualize how you would cope if you got into an accident and were in intense pain. It is quite another when the accident happens, and the doctor tells you that your leg needs to be amputated.

So, what is this training for? The main purpose of the training is to show that, once our initial panic or fear subsides, we have the tools to face life as it is presented to us. The second purpose is to keep these tools available and ready for action when we need them.

Training our mind is like training our body. No matter how good our body is, if we don't train it on a regular basis, it won't function as well as it could. Similarly, even if you understand all the principles of Stoicism, if you don't practice regularly, it won't help you when you need it.

The best way to deal with everyday problems

Stoics believed that a habit is strengthened when you feed it. Walking makes you walk better, running makes you run better. Each time you get angry, it becomes easier for you to get angry again. When you don't feed a habit, it weakens. If you don't want to be bad-tempered, don't feed the habit. Don't do anything that will strengthen the anger habit. Calm down. Don't be angry today. Or the following day.

However, we often forget not to feed the habit. When someone provokes us, we automatically respond with anger. Because of this, the anger habit is strengthened, even if we realize later that we should not have responded angrily.

This week's workout, Stoic Slogans, makes a Stoic principle easy to remember and practice what Epictetus calls a "counter habit." When you keep repeating a slogan often, when a situation arises where you need it, you are more likely to use it because it is there close to you. When you use it, your anger habit weakens. As you keep using it, the anger habit gets weaker and weaker until it becomes just a memory of the way you used to react.

Selected Readings. Week 9

So far in this training program, the readings were mostly by ancient Stoics. They taught us the basic Stoic principles and how to apply them to our lives. The readings in the final two sections are from modern Stoics, people like you and me living their daily lives, to show how these principles are used here and now. All these articles first appeared in THE STOIC magazine.

1. How I used Stoic principles to cope with trauma

[FROM: THE STOIC magazine by Lt. Col. A. Johnson]

How I stumbled onto Stoicism

I am a veteran of the United States Armed Forces diagnosed with Post-Traumatic Stress Disorder (PTSD). In 2017, I joined the Warrior Surf Foundation in an effort to find an alternative way to cope with PTSD outside the traditional options. The foundation is committed to promoting physical and mental wellness for Veterans and their families through adaptive surf therapy and is built around a principle that you cannot go backward in the ocean...you can only look, and move, forward. One of the services provided in the program is individualized coaching sessions focused on unique and specific resiliency measures, which are tailored to each veteran. Andy Manzi, founder of the Warrior Surf Foundation, has been a coach and mentor of mine and we often spoke about happiness—What is it? How do we get it? He introduced me to the book *Unshakable Freedom: Ancient Stoic Secrets Applied to Modern Life* by Chuck Chakrapani. Chakrapani submits "the road to freedom is also the road to happiness." Since then, I've attempted to apply the principles of the book in my journey to healing and my quest to find true happiness. Andy's favorite quote in the book is by Marcus Aurelius: "All the happiness you are seeking by such long, roundabout ways, you can have it all right now...if you leave the past behind you."

This makes happiness seem so simple, yet it's still an everyday challenge. Why?

Stoics give no thought to what they cannot control. When I sat down alone with the book for the first time, I initially believed that Stoics were a gloomy lot of people without feelings based on what I heard in the past. When I thought of the word "stoic" I imagined someone detached and without emotion. I quickly understood that this couldn't be further far from the truth. In reality, Stoics give no thought to problems out of their control, which eliminates unnecessary anguish. I found that by applying Stoic principles discussed in Unshakable Freedom I was more positive, upbeat and able to better enjoy life.

Stoicism is an ancient principle, which the book breaks down for the 21st century reader. Of the six "big ideas" outlined by Chakrapani, three stood out to me. Big Idea #2: leave your past behind, Big Idea #4: where there is fear, freedom is not, and Big Idea #6: life is a festival, enjoy it now.

Big Idea #2: Leave your past behind.
When I first read the words "leave your past behind" I was offended. I felt like forgetting my past would dishonor those that were part of my history and shaped who I am today. What I came to realize, however, was that I didn't have to literally forget my past. I only had to realize that the past was not under my control. If I wanted mental, emotional and spiritual freedom, I would have to let those things go. Once I really grasped the concept, I eventually felt a seismic shift in my thinking. Perhaps leaving my past behind was the BEST way to honor those in my past and strengthen current relationships moving forward.

Big Idea #4: Where there is fear, freedom is not.
"…the Stoic knows that, to the extent you are fearful, you cannot be free." Many returning veterans suffering from PTSD come home with irrational fears and embarrassing behaviors. We are afraid that an event might happen at home that actually happened overseas. We're easily startled, can't handle large crowds, and overreact to loud noises. We

have panic attacks, nightmares, and flashbacks. We shake, sweat, and cry. While bad things happen at home, it's unlikely that we'll experience battlefield-type events at the grocery store or while driving our children to school. These behaviors can make living a normal life very difficult. Just the thought, or the fear of those things happening again where we live and work, can keep us homebound and disassociated. When we live in this state, we clearly have no mental freedom.

Through Unshakable Freedom, I learned that "we develop fearlessness when we become completely aware that certain things are not under our control and, since we can achieve freedom with what we can control, we are not afraid of anything that is not under our control." Leaving fear behind is living freely. It sounds extreme, but I can't control whether a radical terrorist might try to place a roadside bomb along the route to my children's school—not to mention, the sheer unlikelihood that this would actually occur. Therefore, I should not be giving this thought a voice and I should not continue living in fear.

Big Idea #6: Life is a festival. Enjoy it now.
Perhaps this is the biggest idea of them all for veterans seeking personal freedom and happiness. We're often still "living" on the battlefield in our day-to-day lives; living in the past, living in fear, and missing out on being present for the festival before us. While personal freedom remains a daily challenge, I feel more equipped to embrace it, and relish it, today and tomorrow. Using the Stoic principles presented in Unshakable Freedom and through the exercises presented, I, along with many fellow veterans, have found comfort, healing, and newly defined happiness.

Maybe happiness is this: not feeling you should be elsewhere, doing something else, being someone else.

Isaac Asimov

Stoic principles changed my life. I never set out to become a Stoic. I'd venture to say that no veteran has. But I, along with so many of my brothers and sisters in arms, happened upon the Stoic principles explained in Unshakable Freedom and it's changed us all.

Lt.Col. A. Johnson

Lt Col A. Johnson is a United States Air Force veteran.

---

2. Ignore what others think of you

[FROM: THE STOIC magazine by Meredith A. Kunz]
Social media and AI judge us all the time

In the series *Black Mirror,* there's an infamous episode, *Nosedive,* where the main character is judged minute-to-minute by the people around her. Using a social media-style app, the woman's peers add or subtract points to her total. A cascade of missteps, largely beyond her control, results in a lower score—and, as a result, a disturbing downgrade in her real life.

This sounds like a futuristic nightmare, but it's already happening in some countries. Artificial intelligence is quickly combining with facial recognition and social media to become tools of control.

What should a Stoic do?

This situation is of great concern to me as a human being—and as a follower of Stoic practices. It makes me wonder: How can we, as individuals, effectively cope with others' judgments?

Ancient Stoics, with Epictetus the strongest voice among them, teach us that we have no control over what other people think or do, and therefore should ignore others' opinions.

In day-to-day life, this is difficult. People's judgments happen everywhere, and they affect our lives in real ways, costing us jobs, school admittances, relationships, and more.

We are crushed by others' opinions

As a student and a young professional, I'd slave over projects trying to perfect them, working so hard to please others that my own unique imprint got lost. I wanted my efforts to be bulletproof.

But critiques of my work (and of me) inevitably happened. Though I tried to maintain a brave face, I felt crushed inside. That was before I accepted that I couldn't control or change others' reactions, and that I could still live a good life no matter what they thought—before I began practicing a Stoic life philosophy.

Developing core principles

Now, as I have developed a more self-reliant idea about my own value and core principles, I've come to see interactions with others as a dance with an often-unreliable partner.

The ancients knew this. Marcus Aurelius wrote eloquently about what needs to be done: "As humans, we are built to work together in society, and so we must balance our wishes and drives with others." That means we need to put up with people who are separated from reason while still maintaining an inner focus on what we believe in.

So, we have to learn this dance. Even if our feet are often stepped on, bringing involuntary tears to our eyes.

A lifelong project

This is a lifelong project. We can interact with coworkers, gathering input but without letting their agendas penetrate deeply into our ruling centers.

We can learn from mentors yet avoid being controlled by their perspectives—asking ourselves, like Socrates, "Is it true?" We can share what we create, and hope that others will respond to the work as intended or will offer ideas to inform us—but we can't expect this to happen. We can be close with family, yet still follow our own paths.

Living a self-reliant life

The hard truth is that we must learn to ignore how others judge us and endure the consequences. When I feel I am being judged by others, I remind myself: This is yet another opportunity to exercise my core principles—and to live a self-reliant life.

Meredith Alexander Kunz

Meredith Kunz is a Silicon Valley-based writer.

3. Keep your cool while things change

[FROM: THE STOIC magazine by Jonas Salzgeber]

Change is a universal law of nature.

Things are changing constantly. Life is ephemeral—people we care about may be snatched from us in a snap, without warning. This is why Marcus Aurelius often reminded himself of *time* as a river metaphor, in which everything flows past:

> Think often on the swiftness with which the things that exist and that are coming into existence are swept past us and carried out of sight. For all substance is as a river in ceaseless flow, its activities ever changing and its causes subject to countless variations, and scarcely anything stable.

Appreciate without clinging

Things are in constant change, they flow past—new things come and flow past. Therefore, we should remind ourselves how precious our loved ones are—they may soon flow past, too. Let's appreciate what we have now because it might be gone tomorrow. Life is impermanent.

> When giving your child or wife a kiss, repeat to yourself, 'I am kissing a mortal'.
>
> Epictetus

Keep in mind that you are lucky to be able to enjoy the things you have, and that your enjoyment might end abruptly, and that you might never be able to enjoy those things again. Learn to enjoy stuff and people without feeling entitled to them, without clinging.

With the river metaphor in mind, you reduce attachment to what you love, and you diminish the fear of things you're averse to. Because you're aware that all is in constant change, also the things you dislike. You generally reduce the perceived importance of external things.

Knowing that nothing lasts makes you less attached and it becomes easier to accept when things change or when you lose what you love. Epictetus reminds us that when we're attached to a thing like a crystal cup, we should keep in mind what it really is, so that we won't be disturbed when it breaks. He continues:

> So should it be with persons; if you kiss your child, or brother, or friend ... you must remind yourself that you love a mortal, and that nothing that you love is your very own; it is given you for the moment, not forever nor inseparably, but like a fig or a bunch of grapes at the appointed season of the year, and if you long for it in winter you are a fool. So too if you long for your son or your friend, when it is not given you to have him, know that you are longing for a fig in wintertime.

The next time you say goodbye to a loved one, silently remind yourself that this might be your final parting. You'll be less attached to them and if you see them again, you'll appreciate it much more.

Many things that happen to us we cannot change

But we can adopt a noble spirit to bear up bravely with all the changes nature sends our way and bring our will into harmony with reality.

When there are no figs, there are no figs.

Things are in constant change. Become aware of the smallness of this present moment when you're reading this. Whoop, and gone. Compare this moment to the whole day, to the whole week, to your whole lifespan.

Things change, *you* change. Imagine all the people who lived before you. And all the people who will follow when you're gone. Broaden your perspective to the whole history of the human race ...

See? Things come and go. Nothing lasts.

Jonas Salzgeber

Jonas Salzgeber of NJlifehacks.com is the author of The Little Book of Stoicism.

Exercise 9. Stoic Slogans

When to use it

The Stoic Slogans exercise is designed to make it automatic for you to remember a Stoic principle exactly when you need it.

What to use it for

Use it for any Stoic principle which you think would be useful to you, if you consistently applied it to your life. When you are upset about anything for any reason use this technique.

How it works

For example, here are some of my favorites. Start with them or choose your own. Make a list of the ones that appeal to you. Write them down on an index card and carry it with you all the time.

What I don't control is nothing to me.

Who gave the power to others to make me unhappy?

Knowledge is useless if I don't practice it.

There is nothing that I want from anyone.

My anger gives others the power to control me.

Even more powerful are slogans that are funny and evoke powerful imageries. For example,

When you start complaining about reality,

I'm never going to stop the rain by complaining

When you keep using an approach that doesn't work,

Oops, I'm using the wrong handle again!

There goes my cup

Suppose you fret about minor (or even major) things that go wrong in your life. For example, your favorite porcelain cup breaks. The Stoics advised us to remember that it is just a porcelain cup. Eventually porcelain materials will break. So, when it breaks, just say to yourself "Well, it is just a porcelain cup." Then you won't feel so bad. You can keep repeating this phrase whenever something goes wrong. (Massimo Pigliucci uses the phrase, "There goes my cup!" whenever things go wrong.) You may want to apply this phrase to minor things at first— such as losing trivial things. Then, gradually, apply it to larger losses. If someone you know dies, say "There goes my cup." You keep practicing this for several months until it becomes second nature to you, and you can apply it to your job loss or even to the death of your loved one.

Saying "There goes my cup," rather than "Well, it is just a porcelain cup" might work better because "There goes my cup" is not only a light-hearted way of looking at losses, but it also evokes suitable imagery to put your loss in perspective. Here are a few other phrases suggested by Pigliucci:

What do you want, a fig out of season?

Use this slogan when you desire something that is not available at the present moment.

Why won't you do the job of a human being?

Use this slogan whenever you are unwilling to do things that should be done, such as getting up in the morning.

You can take any Stoic principle that appeals to you, make up a slogan, and then use it as often as you can, until the reaction becomes automatic to you. You can of course use more than one slogan at a time. However, it is probably more effective to practice only one slogan until it becomes a habit. Then add another one until that also becomes a habit. And continue this process, adding other slogans.

Some tips for creating and adding slogans

- Make the slogans short. Shorter slogans are easier to remember and repeat.
- Make it light-hearted, if you can. A light-hearted slogan relaxes you, so you are more receptive to the message.
- Make it evoke an image. Slogans like "There goes my cup!" and "Do you want a fig out of season?" can evoke vivid images in our minds thus making the slogans very effective.
- Do not be in a hurry to add slogans. Wait until you make one slogan automatic before adding another.

In their own words

Every habit and faculty is confirmed and strengthened by the corresponding actions, that of walking by walking, that of running by running.

Epictetus, *Discourses* II.18.1 (Chuck Chakrapani, *Stoic Choices*, Ch. 18)

Make a bad beginning and you'll contend with troubles ever after.

Epictetus, *Discourses* II.18.32 (Chuck Chakrapani, *Stoic Choices*, Ch. 18)

Enjoy the Festival of Life

The lesson

Big idea 10. Enjoy the festival of life

Why not enjoy the feast and the pageant while it is given to us to do so?

Epictetus, *Discourses* 4.1 (Chuck Chakrapani, *Stoic Freedom*, Ch. 1)

So far, we have learned how to act rationally, to acquire the special skills needed to achieve happiness, and to deal with everyday problems. We now have everything we need to make our life flow well. Yet, even when we glide through the highway of life smoothly, we may fail to enjoy life to the fullest. We need to learn one final lesson: how not to miss "the festival of life" and to realize that life can not only be happy but also an enjoyable adventure.

The ancient Stoics cautioned us against pursuing pleasures mindlessly. But they also realized there are many enjoyable things in life. They encouraged us to enjoy the good things in life, so long as we don't become dependent on them and don't compromise on the four filters of wisdom, justice, courage, and moderation. They taught us the art of feeling the exhilaration of our drive through life, without losing control over the vehicle.

> If you have understood these things what is there to stop you from living light and living with ease, from gently awaiting anything that may happen, and being content with whatever might have happened?
>
> Epictetus, *Stoic Freedom*, Ch 7 (4.7.)

The way our mind works

We may have everything in life. We may even be very happy with all we have. Yet, soon enough, small dissatisfactions creep in. Maybe your next vacation will bring you joy; maybe the fancy restaurant that you were planning to go to will make you happy. Or the new car. Or something else. If you are not on guard, such minor dissatisfactions have a way of snowballing into major ones. Small discomforts at work can become critical complaints against your job. Minor imperfections in your spouse may become a major justification for divorce.

From an evolutionary perspective, our minds are programmed to seek more, no matter what we have. Billionaires seek even more money. Famous people want even more adulation. Beautiful looking people spend time making themselves look even more beautiful. Getting everything you want in life—including a life that runs smoothly—is not a guarantee that you will enjoy it.

> Even when there is nothing wrong, nor anything certain to go wrong in the future, most humans live in a fever of anxiety.
>
> Seneca, *Epistles*, 13.13

Enjoying what comes our way

When we have everything, our minds look for what we *don't* have. They fail to notice the wonderful things that are all around us. We longingly seek what we don't have and ignore what we have.

If we start noticing, we will begin to see hidden pleasures all around us. The rain drops, the cool morning, the hot sun, the snow, the twilight, the seasons, the way our smart phones work, the way planes fly carrying hundreds of people, the way friends greet each other—in fact, almost everything in life has the potential to make us joyful. Do we even notice these things? No! We get used to them.

Stoics advise us to feel the joy of life as it presents itself. Because Stoics considered pleasures as indifferents, they didn't actively pursue them but were always ready to enjoy what was in front of them. And they asked us to take part in the feast and the pageantry of the festival of life.

> Above all, my friend Lucilius, make this your business: learn how to feel joy.
>
> Seneca. *Moral Essays*. (Translated by J.W. Basore), 161

When things change

We want things to be the same. Yet our life changes constantly. Children grow up to be adults. The government changes. The seasons change. Adults grow into old people. Our good neighbors move to a different part of the city, our friends move to a different state. Our new job is not as much fun as our old job. Our new boss is not as smart as the old one. And old age is not as much fun as youth.

We struggle for a while and get used to the change. But things change again. Our family members or friends die. Our bodies weaken. We resist. We try to control what we cannot control. By now we should know that these are externals and therefore not in our control. If we have been practicing diligently, we can cope with them. We have all the tools.

But we can do better than just cope with changes. We can participate in the festival of life. The way to do this is to not look back on how things were but enjoy what is here now and take pleasure in everything we can. When we learn to enjoy what is in front of us, we will not be concerned about things that we once had but no longer do. We will find many reasons to be joyful. You may not be rich enough to afford the paintings of great artists. How about appreciating the morning sun? How about the wake that follows a boat? Sure, we see a lot of rude people. But we fail to notice how many strangers are kind and helpful to each other.

Is it not enough for you, what you look at every day? Could you have anything better or greater to see than the sun, the moon, the stars, the whole world, the sea?

Epictetus, *Discourses* 2.16.32 (Chuck Chakrapani, *Stoic Choices*, Ch. 16)

We don't own anything

We think that things like our homes, our jobs, our children, and spouses are ours. We think we "own" them. This is why we suffer when they are taken away from us. Instead, think of them as being on loan to you for you to enjoy indefinitely, knowing they can be called back at any time. Once you lose the ownership illusion, you are free to enjoy what is given to you, for however long it is given.

Our world offers endless sources of joy: friends, family, the sunrise, the sunset, the seasons, the wonders of the world, travel. Do not worry about what others think. Enjoy with no guilt, so long as you bear in mind that everything is on loan and can be called back. Even if you face your death, there is no reason not to enjoy what is in front of you.

I must die? If now, I will die now; if in a short time, then I will dine first, because it is dinner time now. When the time comes, I will die.

Epictetus, *Discourses* 1.1.32 (Chuck Chakrapani, *Stoic Foundations*, Ch. 1

Finding joy in everyday things

Where does a Stoic find joy? Everywhere. Whatever is in front of a Stoic has the potential for joy. If that is taken away, the Stoic doesn't feel miserable but looks around to see what else can bring him well-being now. If invited to a party, the Stoic enjoys the company of people. If ignored, he enjoys the solitude. If he can afford it, he enjoys a good meal. If not, a simple sandwich will do fine. A Stoic is always aware of what is available now and enjoys it. She does not complain about yesterday's stale food or tomorrow's potential starvation. Stoics are aware that they don't control the past or the future, so they don't worry about either. If they can do something *now* for a better future, they will. But they are aware that they don't control the future, so they always use what is available to them now to bring them joy.

So, enjoy the festival of life as it is now. If something is taken away from you, don't concern yourself with what you don't have. Enjoy what you have left. As the Stoic Agrippinus said when he learned he was exiled, "Let's go to Aricia and have lunch there!"

If you apply yourself to living only that which you are living—in other words the present—then you can live the rest of your life until your death in peace, benevolence, and serenity.

Marcus Aurelius, *Meditations* (Chuck Chakrapani, *Stoic Meditations* Ch.

Living without regrets or anxiety

Neither the past nor the future are under our control. Therefore, a Stoic does not regret what happened in the past or what she had once because it is already gone. Instead she enjoys whatever is in front of her and under her control with great joy. For the same reason, the Stoic is not anxious about the future either. So long as we are living, so long as we can clearly distinguish what is under our control and what is not, we are free to enjoy the festival of life. It is for us to become aware of the myriad trivial things around us and enjoy what is in front of us. This is Stoic joy.

> If you have understood these things, what is there to stop you from living light and living with ease, from gently awaiting anything that may happen, and being content with whatever might have happened?
>
> Epictetus, *Stoic Freedom*, Ch 7 (4.7.)

Key takeaways

1. Getting everything we want in life is no guarantee that we will enjoy it.
2. Because we long for things, we fail to notice what we already have.
3. We suffer because we don't want things to change.
4. When we realize that we don't own anything, that we are not entitled to anything, then we can enjoy whatever comes our way.
5. Everyday things are joyful, if we start noticing them.
6. Every day is a festival for those who don't believe they don't own anything, but are ready to enjoy whatever is given to them,

Selected readings. Week 10

1. Enjoy what is in front of you right now

[FROM: THE STOIC magazine, written by Flora Bernard]

Not being here

Does it often happen to you that as you are doing something, you also wish you were somewhere else, doing something else? This happened to me last Sunday morning with my three-year old son, a lovely little boy, full of life and energy. At 8 am, he suggested we buy a *pain au chocolat* and go to the nearby park to eat it together in the sun and have fun jumping on the rocks over a small river. Isn't it great that this little boy is excited about the most simple things in life and wants to share them with his mother?

Not enjoying the moment

But I couldn't fully enjoy this moment because my mind was elsewhere. I was thinking of all the work I had to do, but was unable to, because I was alone with my son for the weekend—don't even dream of working with a three-year-old nearby! "I hope he's tired by midday so he can take a nap and I can have two hours free this afternoon", I found myself thinking. It was only 8.30am…

Marcus Aurelius' words came flashing:

Do external things distract you? Then make time for yourself and learn something worthwhile; stop letting yourself be pulled in all directions. People who labor all their lives but have no purpose to direct every thought and impulse toward are wasting their time - even when hard at work.

Marcus Aurelius, *Meditations*, 2.7.

I am physically here with my son, but my mind is elsewhere. I end up being nowhere *truly*.

Lessons learned

So, what is this worthwhile thing I can learn? As far as roles are concerned, it is important for me to be a good mother. That involves spending quality time with my children, playing with them, listening and talking to them, helping them flourish, *being* with them. I even left my cellphone at home that morning so I wouldn't be tempted to check messages and email, as so many other parents do at the playground. But there is one thing I am lacking just now in the park: presence.

Everything is here.

Except me.

I could have asked my parents to take care of my son; I could have organized myself better so as to do this work I had to do *before* the weekend came. That depended on me. But now I'm here.

"Come back", I tell myself. "No one outside of yourself is preventing you from being the mother you want to be. Don't let yourself be distracted."

So, I focus on the little things: the way my son laughs when he jumps and asks me to look at him, the chocolate dripping from his mouth as he enjoys the pastry, all the questions which he is asking me in a continuous flow to understand the world around him.

Who you want to be is always *with* you

Presence is maybe just that: making sure that who I want to be is always *with* me, even in the smallest details of life.

Flora Bernard

Flora Bernard is the co-founder of the philosophy agency, Thae, in Paris France. She is the author of Manager avec les Philosophes (2016).

---

2. If not now, when?

[FROM THE STOIC magazine, written by Ron Pies, MD]
"Don't take life seriously, it's only temporary" (Rabbi Rami Shapiro) is one of those Zen-like teachings that has helped me greatly over the

years, especially in those instances when I have taken life—or myself—too seriously! Of course, on one level, the "temporary" nature of our existence is no laughing matter. But the idea of our non-existence is so utterly incomprehensible to most of us, it may be that gallows humor is the only sane way of coping with our mortality.

Comedian Allen Klein makes some seriously funny observations about the role of humor in dealing with death. He writes,

"Death, dying, and bereavement [are] not funny. Still comedians, cartoonists, and cinematographers show us that it is possible to laugh during times of loss and provide, as Bob Mankoff, the cartoon editor of the New Yorker, says "a little anesthesia of the heart." In seeing demise through humorous eyes, their funny creations not only help us get a different perspective on somber situations but also help us get the upper hand on the inevitable."

As one example of how humor can help us deal with death, Klein cites the 1996 Woody Allen film, *Everyone Says I Love You*, in which "...all the corpses in the funeral home pop out of their coffins dancing and singing "Enjoy Yourself, It's Later than You Think". Among the lyrics of the song are the lines,

Enjoy yourself, it's later than you think
Enjoy yourself, while you're still in the pink
The years go by, as quickly as a wink
Enjoy yourself, enjoy yourself, it's later than you think...

This is good advice, cloaked in the garb of the Borscht Belt *tummler* (comedian/entertainer). Perhaps humor about death and dying is the least frightening way of approaching this often-taboo subject. And, after all, is the advice in the song really so different from that of Hillel the Elder, when he asks,

If not now, when?

Ron Pies, MD

Ron Pies has been studying the similarities among Stoicism, Buddhism, and Judaism. This article is written from that perspective.

3. The festival of life is on. Are we present?

[FROM THE STOIC magazine, written by Chuck Chakrapani]

I have been fortunate enough to travel the world several times and see many wondrous things. But there are also countries I haven't been to and sights I haven't seen. One such sight that I had always wanted to see, but never had the opportunity, was the Northern Lights.

I live in Canada where it is possible to see the Northern Lights, but I need to travel far from where I live and, even if I did, there is no guarantee I would see them when I get there. So, when Iceland Air offered me a free stopover in Iceland on my return journey from London after Stoicon 2018, I took it. Even here there was no guarantee that I would get to see the Northern Lights, but my chances were better, and I didn't have to travel far from Reykjavik.

On the day I landed in Reykjavik, I went to see them, and, to my pleasant surprise, there they were in full force. It was a spectacular sight. We live in a spectacular world. Epictetus called this "the festival of life" and challenged us with this:

Why don't you enjoy the feast and the pageant with others when is given to you to?

"Wait a minute," you may object. "Not everyone is fortunate enough to live in Canada or to get to go Iceland. Where is the festival of life for them?"

The reality is that, for Stoics, every day is a festival, wherever they are. They don't have to go anywhere special, see anything special. They see the beauty of ordinary existence everywhere. Listen to Marcus Aurelius:

A loaf of bread splits open in the oven; random cracks appear on it. These unintended flaws are right and sharpen our appetite. Figs, when they ripen, also crack open. Olives, when they are about to fall just before they decay, appear more beautiful. So are drooping stalks of wheat, wrinkling skin of a staring lion, foam from a wild boar's mouth, and many more such sights.

What Marcus was talking about here was not special pleasures open to him as an emperor or about sights that only a privileged few could see. He was talking about bread splitting open, about drooping stalks of wheat, and about foam from a wild boar's mouth— sights that are open to us all. Are we taking the time to see and appreciate the grace and charm that surrounds us?

The Stoics were so firm in their conviction that even exile couldn't faze them. When Seneca was exiled to Corsica, he consoled his mother Helvia by saying that it was "just a change of place" and went on to say this:

Heavenly things by their nature are always in motion...Don't be surprised, then, if the human mind, which is formed from the same seeds as the heavenly bodies, delights in change and wandering.

For Seneca, his exile is just 'change and wandering' in which the mind takes delight. For the Stoics, every sight is full of charm and grace. Every day is a festival. They are at home wherever they are, doing whatever they are doing.

The festival of life is on right now.

Are we present?

Exercises 10a & 10b

Morning Meditation and Nightly Course Correction

This week we have two exercises. One is the morning meditation and the other is the nightly course correction. The purpose of these two techniques is to remind yourself daily what you have learned and apply it in your everyday life.

a. Morning meditation

When to use it

Morning meditation is best done as soon as you wake up. It prepares you for the day ahead. Use this technique every morning and as needed. Use Morning Meditation to forestall negatively reacting to others when they behave in way that might annoy you. It is also a very pleasant way to start the day.

How it works

When you are up in the morning, continue to lie in bed for a while. Think these thoughts:

1. Give gratitude.

Think of all the things and people you should be thankful for. What have you learnt from others over the years? Who taught you the many things you know now? Your parents, your teachers, your friends, your spouse? Let them come to your mind one by one. Thank them for making you who you are. Who made your life a little better yesterday? The barista at the coffee shop who smiled at you while serving? The supermarket checkout clerk who patiently bagged all your groceries? Let them come to mind. Silently thank them.

2. Prepare for the day.

Continue to lie in bed and say to yourself, "Today I will meet with people who are meddling, unthankful, rude, disloyal, and selfish. People who behave this way don't know the difference between good and evil. But, because I know the difference, I will not be affected by their behavior. Neither will I be angry nor irritated because I'd rather cooperate than fight with others."

Repeat to yourself, "Today I will control only what is under my control. I will not worry about things not in my control." Later in the day, whenever you face any unpleasant encounter, recall these words.

3. Get up cheerfully.

Once you have prepared your mind this way, get up cheerfully. If you are still reluctant to get up, continue your meditation for a while and say to yourself, "I am here to do the work of a human being. Why should I feel I am not up to it and lie in bed? Like every being who does the work assigned to it, I can do the work of a human being too."

In their own words

Giving gratitude.

Marcus Aurelius devotes the first of 12 "books" (chapters) entirely to acknowledging what he received from others. He begins thus: "From grandfather: character and self-control; from father: integrity and manliness," and continues on acknowledging what he learnt from 17 different sources.

Preparing for the day.

Today I shall be meeting with interference, ingratitude, insolence, disloyalty, ill-will, and selfishness—all of them due to the offenders' ignorance of what is good or evil. But for my part, ... (n)either can I be angry with my brother or fall foul of him. To obstruct each other is against Nature's law—and what is irritation or aversion but a form of obstruction.

Marcus Aurelius, *Meditations*, Book (Book 2.1)

Getting up cheerfully.

In the morning, when you have trouble getting out of bed, tell yourself: "I have to go work like a human being, if I am going to do what I was born for ... Or was I created to huddle under the blankets and keep myself warm?

Marcus Aurelius, *Meditations*, Book 5.1

b. The Course Correction technique (End-of-day meditation)

This is a useful technique, used at the end of every day to review how rationally we lived during the day and prepare ourselves better for the following day.

When to use it

Use this technique at the end of every day. This will help you identify instances where you have forgotten to apply the principle of concerning yourself with only things under your control, without worrying about things not under your control.

How it works

Just before going to sleep (or earlier if you prefer) go through the events of the day. Particularly pay attention to events that threatened your freedom: feelings like anger, resentment, fear, and frustration.

Examine how violating Stoic principles by trying to control what is not under your control caused these negative feelings and deprived you of your freedom.

Don't be critical of yourself. Remember also the instances in which you did things that were in line with your freedom. Imagine how you would course-correct using Stoic principles of freedom. Imagine yourself handling it that way if a similar situation arose in the future. If you feel like it, repeat the gratitude part of the morning meditation before going to bed.

In their own words

Every day, we must call upon our soul to give an account of itself ... 'What evils have you cured yourself of today? What vices have you fought? In what sense are you better?' How tranquil, deep, and free it is, when the mind has been praised or warned, and has become the observer and secret judge of its own morals! I make use of this power, and every day I plead my cause before myself... I hide nothing from myself, nor am I indulgent with myself.

Seneca, *Dialogs*, Ch 11

Stoic quotes for the week

Monday

Some are offended if a hairdresser jostles them; they see an insult in surliness of a doorkeeper, the arrogance of an attendant, the haughtiness of a valet. What laughter such things should draw!

Seneca, *On the Constancy of the Wise Man*, 14.1

Tuesday

It is not that we have so little time but that we lose so much ... The life we receive is not short, but we make it so; we are not ill provided but use what we have wastefully.

Seneca, *On the Shortness of Life*

Wednesday

To you everything you have appears small; all my things appear great to me.

Epictetus *Discourses 3.9.21*

Thursday

What [you] can do is not want what you don't have, and cheerfully enjoy what comes your way.

Seneca, *Epistles* 123.4

Friday

Two things we must root out: fear of distress in the future and the memory of distress in the past. The one concerns me no longer. The other concerns me not yet.

Seneca, *Epistles* 78.14

Saturday

If you want, you are free. If you want, you will blame no one, you will accuse no one—if you want everything will happen according to your plan,

Seneca, *Discourses* 1.17.28

Living in the Stoic House

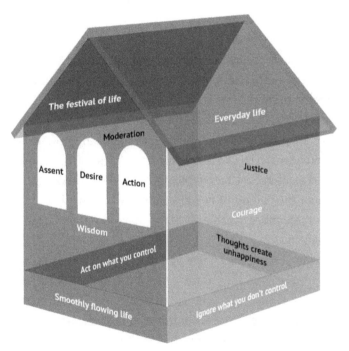

Figure 5 The house metaphor with four foundations, four walls, three windows, and two sloping roofs

Now we have built a Stoic house. The four walls of our house are the four special skills or virtues (Practical wisdom, Justice, Moderation, and Courage), and its three windows are the three Stoic disciplines

181

(Assent, Desire, and Action). The house is protected by the roof sloping in two directions (Living Everyday Life and Enjoying the Festival of Life). And the house is built on the strong foundation of living in accordance with nature using the principle of dichotomy and an understanding of how our thoughts—and not external events—determine our happiness.

We now have all we need to live a life that flows smoothly.

And yet, living a Stoic life is not a matter of just reading a book or even going through a course for 10 weeks or even a year. Just as knowing the rules of the game and having the ability to play it will not make a professional player, so just going through this course will not make you the best Stoic you can be.

So, what do I suggest?

First, repeat the course so you will get the points you might have missed the first time. Repeating the course four or five times will imprint the Stoic principles strongly in your mind.

Second, if any of the exercises (or anything else you might have read elsewhere) are particularly helpful to you, use them as often as needed.

Read Stoic materials that reinforce the basic principles but avoid getting into meaningless and unpleasant arguments about Stoic principles. Remember, you don't need to convince anyone that these principles are correct and workable. If others have different opinions about things, let them.

By the way, I recommend that you read THE STOIC magazine published by The Stoic Gym. As I write this, it is free (https://www.thestoicgym.com/the-stoic-subscribe/) and many prominent and less prominent Stoics contribute to this magazine. It is beautifully put together and often fun to read. The articles are short and practice oriented.

I wish you all the best.

Chuck

The Stoic Gym Publications
(Free and Regular)

FREE MAGAZINE
THE STOIC: The Journal of the Stoic Gym

THE STOIC is the official online magazine of The Stoic Gym. It is an applied magazine designed to bring high quality articles on how to live a life of happiness, serenity, and freedom using Stoic principles. By subscribing, you can have the magazine delivered to your inbox, as soon as an issue is published. Subscribe. *It's FREE!* *https://www.thestoicgym.com/the-stoic-subscribe/*

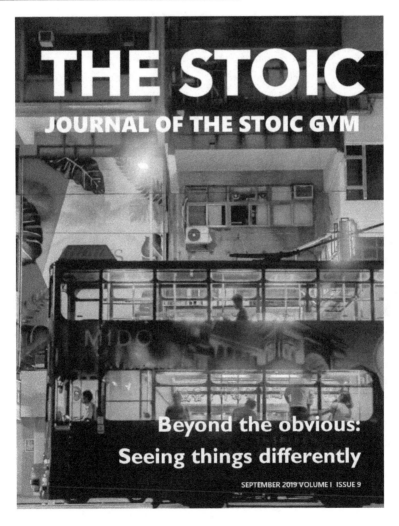

THE STOIC

JOURNAL OF THE STOIC GYM

Beyond the obvious:
Seeing things differently

SEPTEMBER 2019 VOLUME I ISSUE 9

FREE ONLINE BOOKS FROM THE STOIC GYM
THE GOOD LIFE HANDBOOK

The Good Life Handbook is a rendering of Epictetus' Enchiridion in plain English. It is a concise summary of the teachings of Epictetus, as transcribed and later summarized by his student Flavius Arrian. The Handbook is a guide to the good life. It answers the question, "How can we be good and live free and happy, no matter what else is happening around us?" Ancient Stoics lived in a time of turmoil under difficult conditions. So, the solutions they found to living free were tested under very stringent conditions. For example, Epictetus was a lame slave who made himself free and happy later in life by following the principles set out in this book. Available **FREE** on Amazon for Kindle https://amzn.to/2FNXnhr

A FORTUNATE STORM

Strange is the story of Stoicism. Three unconnected events—a shipwreck in Piraeus, a play in Thebes, and the banishment of a rebel in Turkey—connected three unrelated individuals to give birth to a philosophy. It was to endure two thousand years and offer hope and comfort to hundreds of thousands of people along the way.
Stoicism had seven formal leaders or "scholarchs," but much of what we know of Stoicism today comes from four Stoics who lived after the all the scholarchs were gone. This is the story of those eleven people.
Many others contributed to Stoicism, but to make this brief and readable, Dr. Chuck Chakrapani tells the story of Stoicism through these eleven leading figures of Stoicism. Available **FREE** at The Stoic Gym https://www.thestoicgym.com/fortunate-storm-free/ (Also available in print on Amazon *https://amzn.to/2W37MLI*)\\

UNSHAKABLE FREEDOM

How can we achieve total personal freedom when we have so many obligations and so many demands on our time? Is personal freedom even possible? Yes, said the Stoics and gave us a blueprint for freedom. Dr Chakrapani brings their teachings to the digital era.

WHAT READERS ARE SAYING

You'll "probably get through it in a few hours, enjoy the whole thing, and come away with an accurate and workable idea of Stoic philosophy. So please do just go and read it."

Donald Robertson, Book Reviews—Stoicism

"If you want to apply [the Stoic principles] right away, it is a wonderful book for that. This will help a lot of people. This is a gateway book."

Dr. Gregory Sadler, Sadler's Honest Book Reviews.

Dr. Chakrapani has written a superbly helpful book."

Broga, **Amazon** (UK)

The absolute best book by far … It explains Stoicism in an extremely accessible and easy to understand format. Highly recommended. I've gifted it to quite a few people.

Illegalutrun, **reddit/r/stoicism**

Available on all online bookstores (eBook or paperback)

https://amzn.to/2Eb8zU7

THE COMPLETE WORKS OF MUSOINUS RUFUS

Musonius Rufus, the man who taught Epictetus, has something to say on everything. A man far ahead of his time, he was a minimalist. vegetarian, proto-feminist, minimalist, and more. *https://amzn.to/2WbWwN1*

THE COMPLETE WORKS OF EPICTETUS:
A set of five indispensable books

Stoic Foundations (Discourses Book 1) explains the basic tenets of Stoicism. If you are interested in Epictetus' teachings, this is where you should start.

Stoic Choices is the plain English version of Discourses Book 2. It discusses what our choices are in life and how to make better choices.

Stoic Training is the third book of Discourses of Epictetus in plain English. Stoics did not only believe in theoretical knowledge but held it as critical that we practice what we learned.

Stoic Freedom (Discourses Book 4) focuses on freedom. Personal freedom is close to Epictetus' heart, and his rhetoric shines when he talks about freedom. But, what does a free person look like?

Stoic Inspirations is basically a summary (or extracts) from the above four books by Arrian (Enchirdion) and The Golden Sayings of Epictetus. It also includes 'fragments' (quotes) as well as a biography.

Available in print and digital editions from Amazon at *https://amzn.to/2CGY3lk*

THE COMPLETE WORKS OF MARCUS AURLIUS

 *Meditations* is the personal journal kept by the beloved Roman Emperor Marcus Aurelius. It was never meant for publication and yet, after his death, it has become probably the most widely read book on Stoic philosophy. Meditations is a deeply moving personal journal which is uplifting and invigorating. **https://amzn.to/2DqLLiT**

 While Meditations is one of the best-read Stoic books, not many of us know about Marcus' other writings: his personal letters and speeches. For the first time ever *Aurelius, the Unknown* presents all his letters *and speeches in a single volume. Also includes a biographic sketch and several anecdotes from his life. A must-read for all fans of Marcus Aurelius.*

https://amzn.to/2DqLLiT

THE AUTHOR

Dr. Chuck Chakrapani is Editor of THE STOIC magazine, and author of about fifteen books on Stoicism.

Chuck is a psychologist by training, a data scientist by profession, and a Stoic author by choice. A prolific writer, he has written over 25 books and 500 articles on different subjects ranging from investment strategies, marketing research, psychology, statistics, analytics and Stoicism.

You can reach him at TheStoic@TheStoicgym.com

CPSIA information can be obtained
at www.ICGtesting.com
Printed in the USA
LVHW040147151019
634128LV00008B/2618/P